W9-BGI-347

9/95

FIRST AND SECOND
THESSALONIANS

FIRST AND SECOND THESSALONIANS

by

CHARLES CALDWELL RYRIE

MOODY PRESS

CHICAGO

COPYRIGHT ©, 1959, BY
THE MOODY BIBLE INSTITUTE
OF CHICAGO

ISBN: 0-8024-2052-4

Moody Press, a ministry of the Moody Bible Institute, is designed for education, evangelization and edification. If we may assist you in knowing more about Christ and the Christian life, please write us without obligation to: Moody Press, c/o MLM, Chicago, Illinois 60610.

Printed in the United States of America

CONTENTS

BACKGROUNDS

FIRST AND SECOND THESSALONIANS are probably Paul's first extant epistles. Indeed, they are among the earliest of all the New Testament writings. Although penned so early these epistles in no way reflect undeveloped, immature teaching, for Paul had been a Christian for seventeen or eighteen years by the time he wrote I Thessalonians, and he had been a missionary for seven or eight years. His theology was fully developed in his mind and tested in his experience before he ever penned an epistle.

The Epistles are like finely cut gems. They reflect the depths of theological thought, especially in the area of future things; they mirror the pattern of teaching which the apostle used with new Gentile converts; from every part shine forth the character and conduct of Paul's missionary heart; they sparkle with the brilliance of the captivating power of the gospel of the grace of Christ. They are a joy to read and a delight to study.

I. THE CITY OF THESSALONICA

In Paul's day Thessalonica (now Salonika) was an important city. Its history had made it so, for in 315 B.C. Cassander, son of Antipater, reconstructed Therma (named for its hot springs) into a fine metropolis and gave it the name of Thessalonica after his wife, who was the daughter of Philip of Macedon and half-sister of Alexander. Under the Romans the city was the capital of the newly formed province and its largest city with a population of about 200,000. Its location also contributed to its importance. It was one of the greatest, if not the greatest, of the cities along the entire Egnatian Road, a great military highway which connected Rome with the east and which ran parallel to the sea line of communication by way of Corinth. Situated at the northwestern corner of the Aegean Sea, its sheltered harbor was made into a naval station and equipped with docks by the Romans. Its location midway between the Adriatic and the Hellespont makes it even today a natural outlet for traffic from all points.

This commercial activity had two important results. First, it made Thessalonica a wealthy city. Well-to-do Romans settled there, and Jewish merchants were attracted by the commercial advantages of the city (Acts 17:4). However, the majority of people, as everywhere, made their living by manual labor. Macedonian women, though, did enjoy a higher social position and greater privileges than elsewhere in the civilized world. Second, it brought Thessalonica a reputation for evil and licentiousness. The strange mixtures of a seaport city and the rites of the worship of the Cabiri necessitated a special appeal on the part of the apostle for chaste living (I Thess. 4:1-8).

Thessalonica was a free city and enjoyed autonomy in all its internal affairs. Although it was the residence of the provincial governor, he exercised no civil authority, the city being ruled by politarchs (cf. Luke's accurate reporting in Acts 17:6). This political privilege was jealously guarded by the people, who were extremely sensitive about anything that might result in imperial disfavor. Therefore, the charge of treason framed against Paul and his companions was the most dangerous that could have been laid against them in such a city (Acts 17:7).

II. THE WORK AT THESSALONICA

To this city on his second missionary journey came Paul, accompanied by Silas and Timothy. Silas had been chosen in Antioch as Paul's partner for this second journey after the separation from Barnabas over John Mark. Young Timothy was enlisted at Lystra (Acts 16:1-3) after the journey had begun. Having revisited the churches established on the first journey (which was the original purpose of the trip), they came to an impasse at Troas until Paul had the vision of the man of Macedonia calling him to come to Europe to help him. Their first European stop was Philippi, but they were compelled to leave after the illegal imprisonment experience. They then traveled the hundred miles to Thessalonica where Paul, as was his custom, preached in the synagogue for three Sabbaths with success (Acts 17:2). The converts included Jews and a great multitude of devout Greeks who were attracted by the monotheism and morality of Judaism and who had attached themselves to the synagogue. Some of the believers were of the upper classes, but most were apparently of the working class, since Paul refused to be dependent financially on them in any way.

Naturally the Jewish community did not like to be depleted in this manner, so some of the Jews resorted to violence by inciting a mob to attack the house of Jason, Paul's host, and drag him before the rulers where he was charged with harboring traitors to Caesar. This charge of treason is the first recorded after the trial of Jesus before Pilate and could have been an outgrowth of the eschatological preaching of Paul at Thessalonica as reflected in the Epistles. The politarchs took security of Jason and the others accused with him and let them go. Probably this action was in the nature of placing them under a peace bond which included the guarantee that Paul would leave the city immediately and not return.

From Thessalonica the missionaries proceeded to Berea, but soon were compelled to leave there because of opposition from the Thessalonian Jews who dogged their steps. Paul went on to Athens, where Timothy joined him and from where he was dispatched back to Thessalonica in order to report on the condition of the young church. Both Timothy and Silas rejoined Paul at Corinth, from which city the two Epistles to the Thessalonians were written.

The duration of Paul's stay in Thessalonica is the subject of debate. Acts 17:2 declares that Paul reasoned in the synagogue for three (apparently successive) Sabbaths, while I Thessalonians 2:7-11 mentions the fact that he was in Thessalonica long enough to gain employment and Philippians 4:16 seems to imply that he was there long enough to be able to receive two gifts of money from the Philippians. Because of the apparent teaching of these latter two passages, many are certain that Paul had to be in Thessalonica over a period of months — certainly longer than three or four weeks.

For instance, Ramsay (*St. Paul the Traveler and Roman Citizen,* p. 228) thinks Paul was there six months. However, the anxious tone of I Thessalonians makes it quite clear that Paul was not there long enough to see the church established but rather that he was forced to leave the city before little more than the work of evangelizing had been done. As for his working during the stay in the city, this could easily have been necessary even if he stayed only a month and especially if he assumed some or all of the maintenance of Silas and Timothy as well. A careful study of Philippians 4:16 would indicate that it probably does not mean that Paul received several gifts from the Philippians while at Thessalonica. The verse may be translated this way: "Both (when I was) in Thessalonica and (*kai*) more than once (*hapax kai dis*) (when I was in other places) you sent . . ." (cf. Morris, *The Epistles of Paul to the Thessalonians,* p. 17). Thus the verse need not imply that any more than one gift reached Paul in Thessalonica. Therefore, we conclude that there is no definite reason for extending Paul's stay in Thessalonica past the month indicated by the Book of Acts.

III. DATE AND PLACE OF WRITING

As has been stated, both Epistles were written from Corinth during the apostle's eighteen-month

stay in that city. The first Epistle was written during the earlier part of that period just after Timothy had returned from Thessalonica with news of the progress of the church, and the second letter was dispatched a matter of weeks (or at the most a few months) later. Any date assigned will have to be approximate, though probably the writing of these letters should be placed during the winter of A.D. 51-52.

IV. PURPOSE OF FIRST THESSALONIANS

First Thessalonians was written after the receipt of Timothy's favorable report of his visit to the city. Therefore, its first purpose is to express Paul's thankfulness and give encouragement to the people. Second, Paul in this Epistle defends himself against what was evidently a campaign of the Jewish opponents of Christianity to defame and slander him. They had apparently spread the word that Paul's conduct was dishonorable and that his failure to return to the city proved that he was only interested in whatever profit he could gain from his evangelistic mission in the town. The first three chapters of the Epistle contain Paul's answer to these charges, which may have had some success among the people. Not to have defended himself would have been disastrous to the entire missionary enterprise in all of Macedonia.

A third purpose of the letter was to encourage

these new converts to stand fast in the face of persecutions and pressure to revert to the easy standards of the paganism from which they had turned. Fourth, a doctrinal question had arisen in the church concerning the fate of Christians who had died before the ushering in of Christ's kingdom. This Paul answers in the fourth chapter. Finally, some matters in relation to their church life had to be dealt with. Some of the believers needed to be reminded that although Christianity is a religion of charity, they were not to be moochers. In their church services, too, there was some misunderstanding concerning their relationship to the work and gifts of the Holy Spirit and to one another in the congregation.

This is a letter from a pastor who was basically satisfied and even thrilled with the progress of his flock but who wanted to encourage them to go on in their faith. It is a heart-warming letter showing a side of Paul which we do not see in some of his other Epistles.

V. PURPOSE OF SECOND THESSALONIANS

The purpose of the second Epistle can be discovered from the letter itself. In one way or another information had reached Paul concerning the state of the church in Thessalonica. Good word came concerning their steadfastness in persecution and for this Paul commends the believers. However, there had been misapprehension, if not misrepresentation, of the apostle's teaching concerning the coming of the Day of the Lord. Some thought it had evidently begun and that they were experiencing its judgments when the apostle had taught them in the first Epistle that they were not appointed unto that wrath. Concerning this Paul corrects them. Finally, the brief warning of the first Epistle (5:14) against disorderly conduct had had little effect and the situation had worsened. Concerning this Paul gives strict and definite instructions. He is careful to give whatever praise was deserved, while at the same time dealing firmly and clearly with the deviations in doctrine and practice.

FIRST THESSALONIANS

Salutation, 1:1
I. PERSONAL AND HISTORICAL, 1:2—3:13
    A. PAUL'S COMMENDATION OF THE
       THESSALONIANS, 1:2-10
       1. *The content of his commendation, 1:2-8*
          a. Their work of faith, 3a, 4-5
          b. Their labor of love, 3b, 8
          c. Their patience of hope, 3c, 6-7
       2. *The confirmation of his commendation, 1:9-10*
          a. Thessalonians' faith confirmed, 9b
          b. Thessalonians' love confirmed, 9c
          c. Thessalonian's hope confirmed, 10
             (1) The character of their hope

17

THE SALUTATION

FIRST-CENTURY LETTERS began sensibly. Instead of requiring the reader to look at the end to find the signature, they began with the name of the writer, the recipient, and some sort of greeting. First Thessalonians is no exception.

It is always interesting to observe how a man introduces himself. Sometimes Paul speaks of himself as an apostle (Gal. 1:1), sometimes as a servant (Rom. 1:1), but here without any additional descriptive word. He does, however, associate himself with Silas and Timothy (the latter appearing in ten of Paul's Epistles) not as co-authors but as a matter of courtesy since they were with Paul during the mission in Thessalonica. The name *Paul* means "little" and was the Roman name given him at birth along with his Jewish name *Saul*. It was common practice among the Jews to give a child both a Jewish and Gentile name, and particularly would this have been natural with Paul whose father was a Roman citizen. The Jewish name,

Saul, is used until his ministry turns to the Gentiles (Acts 13:9), after which his Gentile name, Paul, is appropriately used.

The recipients of the letter are designated as the "church of the Thessalonians." The form of address is unique, for usually Paul says "to the church in such-and-such a place," and the difference emphasizes Paul's individual interest in each member of this church. The position of these believers, while locally in Thessalonica and circumstantially in persecution, was spiritually in God the Father and the Lord Jesus Christ. The oneness of the Father and the Son as well as the oneness of believers with the Godhead is affirmed.

Paul's greeting is "Grace be unto you and peace" (the remainder of the verse as found in the King James Version is absent from the best manuscripts). Grace, akin to the word *joy,* is that which causes joy, and in a Christian sense it means the undeserved favor of God toward the sinner in providing the free gift of salvation through the death of Christ. Peace to us today means the absence of war; but in the Old Testament it meant harmony between man and God and the resultant wholeness and prosperity of the soul. As used here it of course has that Old Testament flavor with the Christian additive that the harmony was made possible through the death of Christ. The order of the two words is significant, for there can be no real peace until grace has been experienced in the heart.

I

PERSONAL AND HISTORICAL
1:2 — 3:13

A. PAUL'S COMMENDATION OF THE THESSALONIANS, 1:2-10

1. *The Content of His Commendation, 1:2-8*

IT WAS ALSO CONVENTIONAL in ancient letters to open with a word of gratitude. Paul's commendation of his readers, however, is no matter of following convention, but it is a genuine expression of his feeling for them (cf. Gal. 1:6 where there is no such word) and an attempt to raise their thoughts to God on whom was their dependance. The regularity of his thanksgiving for them (as expressed in the words *always* and *without ceasing*) also shows that this was no mere perfunctory matter with him. Paul was practicing what he preached when he prayed for them "without ceasing" (this is the same word used in 5:17). The three particular things for which Paul was thankful are the subject of the discussion of the remainder of the chapter.

a. Their work of faith, 3a, 4-5. The first of these three things for which Paul gives thanks is the work of faith. This could refer to the initial act of faith which brought salvation to the Thessalonians, or it may refer to the work which followed that act of saving faith. Probably the reference is to the latter and thus comprehends the whole Christian life work, but of course the initial act of faith from which all good works spring is in the background of this meaning.

Because of the fact that their faith exhibited itself in good works, Paul was certain that they belonged to God's elect. They were those who were beloved of God. The word *beloved* is a perfect participle, which means that God's love existed in the past and continues on to the present with unabated force. Election proceeds from this love of God for His chosen ones.

It is sometimes said that one cannot know whether or not another is elect, but here Paul claims that very knowledge. His reasons are stated in verse 5, and they are related to the way the gospel came to the Thessalonians during his evangelistic mission in their city. There are three characteristics. The first is negative — "not in word only"; that is, not in any power that could come through eloquence of speech. By contrast, the second characteristic was that it did come in power. Evidently Paul is not referring to miracles accompanying the preaching of the gospel at Thessalonica (this would require the use of the plural of the word *power*) but to the sincerity and simplicity of the message as empowered by the Holy Spirit. Words, however eloquent, cannot change man's heart, but the Spirit using the preached message can and does (cf. John 16:7-11). The third characteristic of the work of faith was that it brought to the three missionaries complete assurance of the effectiveness of the message which they had preached. "Much assurance" is closely connected with the Holy Spirit (for there is no repetition of "in" before "much assurance") and means the confidence which the Spirit brought to the hearts of both the evangelists and the converts. For confirmation of what he has just asserted concerning his preaching Paul appeals in the last part of verse 5 to the knowledge of his readers.

b.   Their labor of love, 3b, 8. The second thing for which the apostle commends his readers is their labor of love. The word which Paul uses for labor in verse 3 means "fatiguing work," and differs from the word *work* in the phrase *work of faith* in that it includes the cost associated with the labor. Love is that which seeks the highest good in the one loved, and since the greatest good one can do for an unredeemed person is to bring him the gospel, a labor of love would mean the sounding out of the word of the Lord. This the Thessalonians did to the point of fatigue (cf. Rev. 14:13) in Macedonia, Achaia, and every place (v. 8). The word translated "sounded out" is very picturesque. The Greek letters simply changed into English characters spell our word *echo*. Thus the picture is of the message of the gospel so stirring the strings of the Thessalonians' hearts that it reverberated in strong and clear tones to all Greece and everywhere. That which was sounded out was the word of the Lord, a phrase which is "used here with direct reference to the Gospel-message ('a word having the Lord for its origin, its centre, and its end')" (Milligan, *St. Paul's Epistles to the Thessalonians*, p. 12). The exact phrase is used elsewhere by Paul with the same meaning only in II Thessalonians 3:1. This is the only church Paul calls a pattern, not only to the heathen but to other Christians, for to labor in sending forth the gospel is the greatest work of love anyone can perform.

c. Their patience of hope, 3c, 6-7. The third thing for which the converts are commended is their patience of hope. The word translated "patience" in verse 3 is *hupomonē*. It does not denote a negative and passive resignation to persecution or problems, but rather a positive and optimistic fortitude in spite of indignities suffered. The Christian's confident expectation is in his Lord and particularly in the return of the Lord. This same idea concerning our hope is emphasized in the first chapter of the second Epistle.

Such hope always shines brightest in the midst of persecution, and the Thessalonians knew much about this even in their short Christian experience. They had been under such pressure and affliction that Paul likens their case to his own and to the Lord's (v. 6). But their suffering was accompanied by joy inspired by or originating from the Holy Spirit (the genitive "of the Holy Ghost" is that of source — a joy which comes from the Spirit). The Christian is never promised a crown of roses (cf. John 16:33), but with affliction he may always experience joy which the Holy Spirit brings to his heart (cf. John 16:22).

Because of this the Thessalonians became examples to other believers in Greece (v. 7). The word *example* is *tupos,* from which we get the English word *type.* It originally meant the mark of a blow (cf. John 20:25); then it came to mean the figure formed by the blow; and thus its resultant meaning is "image" or "pattern" (Heb. 8:5). The meaning, then, is that the conduct of these believers served as a pattern for other Christians in the two provinces of Greece: Macedonia (the northern part of Greece, of which Thessalonica was the chief city) and Achaia (the southern part of Greece, of which Corinth, the place of writing of the letter, was the principal city).

2. *The Confirmation of His Commendation,* 1:9-10

Paul makes a very daring statement in verse 9. He says in effect that anybody (both Christian and heathen) could tell what is going on in Thessalonica, so active was the group there. It was not merely a matter of the missionaries' commending the church, but anyone you might ask would say the same thing.

a. Thessalonians' faith confirmed, 9b. Their faith was confirmed by those around them who continually (the verb *show* is present tense) testified to the fact that these Christians were different because they turned to God from idols. The phrase *turned to God* also shows that the majority of the church were from a Gentile, not a Jewish, background.

b. Thessalonians' love confirmed, 9c. Their labor of love in disseminating the gospel is confirmed in the phrase *to serve the living and true God.* The word *serve* really means to serve as a slave, and the Old Testament picture of the per-

petual bondslave is in Deuteronomy 15:16 ff. In
our Lord's humiliation He took "the form of a
slave" (Phil. 2:7), and Paul too delights to call
himself a slave of Jesus Christ (Rom. 1:1). Truly
these Thessalonians did become followers of him
and of the Lord (v. 6) in willing slavery to Christ
their Master.

c.　Thessalonians' hope confirmed, 10.

(1)　The character of their hope. That patient
endurance of hope is expressed in verse 10 by
the word *wait*. Actually the Greek word is a compound of the usual word for "wait" preceded by
a preposition which intensifies the idea, but which
also means "up," when standing by itself. Thus we
may capture that intensive meaning by actually
translating the preposition as part of the meaning
of the verb. The meaning is: they were waiting
up for their Lord. Do you not see the outlook of
expectancy, triumphant hope, and constant endurance displayed in the attitude of waiting up?

(2)　The content of their hope. Their waiting
up was for a person, and as Christians we wait
not so much for an event as for a person.

(3)　The center of their hope. That person for
whom we wait up is identified in three ways. He
is the Son, the Divine One. He is Jesus, the human
one. He is the Deliverer from the wrath to come,

and that deliverance is complete, for it is out of (*ek*) the coming wrath.

This was the report of those who lived with the believers and who watched their lives day by day, as well as those who lived in distant regions and heard of their witness second-hand. It is a convincing testimony to the power of the gospel to change lives, which power has not diminished over the centuries and which testimony ought to be just as clear today.

B. Paul's Conduct Among the Thessalonians, 2:1-12

Paul now returns to the subject he briefly touched on in the last part of 1:5, his conduct during the mission in Thessalonica. He appeals to his readers to affirm the truth of what he is going to say in this chapter. The word *yourselves* is in an emphatic position in the Greek sentence. He calls on them to testify that his entrance among them did not prove to be in vain (from *kenē*, empty, void of power). This is a daring thing for a man to do, for Paul is saying in effect, "Ask anybody in Thessalonica; they'll tell you that I'm telling the truth when I say that I behaved holily, justly, and unblamably all the time I was in the city." In these first twelve verses lies the secret of Paul's success as a servant of Christ.

1.   *Conduct Characterized by Unselfish Love,*
2:1-4

a.   Negative aspect of his love, 2. Paul's conduct
did not include any love of self or of personal
comforts. To prove this he cites what happened
to him and his party at Philippi. There they had
been subjected to both physical suffering ("suffered before") and mental torture ("shamefully
entreated"), for they had undergone the affliction
of beating and imprisonment, and they had en-
dured indignities from which Roman citizens were
exempt. It was unlawful to strip, beat, and im-
prison Roman citizens without a hearing, but in
spite of the fact that this had happened to Paul
at Philippi, and in spite of the fact that it might
have happened again at Thessalonica, that did not
deter him from preaching the gospel boldly in the
latter city. Boldness is a compound of two words
which mean "all speech." Therefore, basically it
means freedom of speech and the resultant confidence which comes from such freedom (cf. Acts
26:26; Eph. 3:12). This boldness is the result of
no mere natural courage but a supernatural en-
ablement, for it is "boldness in our God."

b.   Positive aspects of his love, 3-4. On the
other hand Paul's conduct among them was ab-
solutely pure and approved of God. The fact that
Paul evidently found it necessary to mention this

implies that he had been charged with deceiving conduct. It was not uncommon for preachers of strange cults to seek only their own financial profit, and apparently Paul had been classed as one of these.

(1) Love of the truth, 3. Paul could boldly exhort people to receive the gospel of God for three reasons. (a) First, he was assured that the gospel did not have its source in error ("not of deceit" — *planē* means "error," not "deceit). The early missionaries of the cross knew that they were not victims of a great deception or lie. The facts and purpose of Christ's life, death, and resurrection were and are true. (b) Second, the secret of the gospel was not in its appeal to uncleanness. It may seem strange to us to realize that Paul felt it necessary to disclaim sensuality, but the success of heathen religions could often be traced to their sanction of immorality. Paul's message had evidently been charged with such, and he makes it clear that Christianity did not require licentious rites in order to promote it as the cults did. (c) Third, the sending of the truth was not with impure motives. Paul loved the truth because it did not require guile to convince. The word *guile* is from a word which means "bait" and thus signifies any crafty design or catching. The preposition here is different from that in the preceding

two phrases. The source of Paul's exhortation was not from (*ek*) error nor from (*ek*) uncleanness, nor was it in (*en*) the atmosphere of deceit. Who can help loving a message like this? And yet it is this very love that many Christians do not have, and that is why they find it difficult to witness.

(2) Love of the task, 4. Paul not only loved the truth; he also loved the work. This is proved by the fact that he had been approved of God over the years. The word translated "allowed" means "to test, prove" and thus "approve," and it is in the perfect tense, which shows that Paul is referring to the entire span of his Christian life up to this time. He was approved of God during his three-year isolation in Arabia (Gal. 1:17). He was further approved during the seven or eight years he had to spend in Tarsus after returning from Arabia (cf. Acts 9:30; 11:25). This must have been very difficult for the Christian man who had left home some twenty years before to study in Jerusalem to be a rabbi. He proved himself further on the first missionary journey through disappointment (when John Mark left the party, Acts 13:13), danger (when he was stoned at Lystra, Acts 14:19), and dispute (at the Jerusalem council, Acts 15). In all the tests God had given him he had proved himself faithful and could therefore speak in this confident manner of God's approval

on his ministry. In this assurance of past approval Paul was speaking to the Thessalonians (present tense). Too, it was because he realized that it is God who gives approval that he did not aim his ministry at pleasing men but God who proves (this is the same word as translated "allowed" in the first part of the verse) the heart. It is always a temptation to gear our message to that which pleases men, and to aim our methods at that which will not displease them in any way. This Paul did not do.

2. *Conduct Characterized by Unstinting Labor,* 2:5-9

a. Labor in selflessness, 5-6. Paul's unselfish labor at Thessalonica was characterized as being free from three things. (1) It was free from undue influence. The sense of the word translated "flattering" is difficult to convey, for it has the idea of using the kind of acceptable speech which lulls another person into a false sense of security in order that the speaker may gain his own ends. Our English word *cajolery* is similar. (2) It was free from covetousness. Paul did not seek from his converts anything unfairly. Covetousness is not only the desire for money but for self-promotion, and this Paul emphatically disclaims in his evangelizing of Thessalonica. Indeed he explains later on (v. 9) how he labored in order to give the gos-

pel to them freely. To attest this he appeals to
God as his witness since it was impossible for his
readers to see what was in his heart. He is claiming
more than that his actions were free from covetousness; his heart was free from such too, and God
bore him witness in that. (3) It was free from self-
glory. To glorify is to manifest or show off. Paul
disclaims that he ever sought that men should
show him off. Paul has obtained honor of men,
but he never looked for praise from men.

    b.   Labor with gentleness, 7. Rather than try-
ing to make gain from the Thessalonians, Paul
and his companions were gentle among them. The
exact reading of verse 7 is difficult to determine.
The word *gentle* (*ēpioi*) is spelled in Greek ex-
actly the same way as the word *babe* (*nēpioi*) with
the exception of the first letter, which also happens
to be the last letter of the preceding word. The
manuscript evidence gives some preference to the
word *babe,* while *gentle* seems to make better
sense. Since the evidence is fairly evenly divided,
and since it is not difficult to account for altering
the original either way, it is not easy to choose
between "we were gentle" and "we were babes." In
either case the preachers treated the people with
tenderness and without any trace of superiority.

    Concerning the figure of a nurse cherishing her
children there is no manuscript question. Since

the children are "her own children" (the reflexive pronoun is in the text), most likely the nurse is also the mother, and thus we should understand the word *nurse* to mean "nursing mother." Her action is one of cherishing, or caring for her children with extreme tenderness. The word *cherish* means "to warm" and is used of the way a mother bird covers her young (Deut. 22:6); its only other occurrence in the New Testament is of our Lord's relationship to His church (Eph. 5:29). The picture Paul paints of his labors is very vivid and evidently in sharp contrast to the one his opponents were slanderously ascribing to him.

c. Labor with willingness, 8-9. Utmost willingness also characterized the ministry in Thessalonica. This was motivated by Paul's deep yearning to see them saved (the word *affectionately desirous* is rare and probably means a mother's yearning over her child, cf. the Septuagint of Job 3:21 for the only other occurrence). Such strong motivation brought continuous willingness (the verb is in the imperfect tense, signifying continuousness) to give everything ("their own souls") for their converts. It was the unreserved abandonment which was the secret of Paul's effectiveness. There was no holding back of anything, and he asks the Thessalonians to remember that he worked night and day in order that he could support himself

and his party financially and give the gospel to
them without charge. Undoubtedly some of the
chief women of the city and perhaps Jason too had
money, and we know that the church sent Paul
money later on (cf. Phil. 4:16); nevertheless, during the period of evangelization he would not receive their financial support. No one could charge
him with greed. This is the secret of Paul's success — the continual and selfless giving of his all
to people whom he loved dearly.

3. *Conduct Characterized by Unspotted Life,*
2:10-12

a. The excellency of Paul's life, 10. Paul now
speaks of the unspotted testimony of his own life,
and since it was a matter of both inward and outward observation, he calls both his readers and
God to witness the truth of what he is about to
claim. While some commentators have emphasized
that "holily" refers to Paul's conduct in relation
to God, "justly" in relation to man, and "unblamably" in relation to self, it seems better to recog-
nize the three adverbs as describing completely
the apostle's conduct in all its relationships. "Holily" means "religiously"; "justly" means "righteous-
ly"; "unblamably," "without fault or cause for re-
proach." This must have been a true and accurate
description of Paul's conduct; otherwise he would

not have called so confidently on the believers to affirm his testimony.

b. The exhortation of Paul's life, 11. Exhortation must be backed up by excellency of life, and Paul reminds the believers how paternally he dealt with them. The figure of a paternal relationship with believers appears only in Paul's Epistles and only in connection with the conversion experience (cf. I Cor. 4:14; II Cor. 6:13; Gal. 4:19; Philem. 10). Like a father, Paul was very careful and wise in his dealings with these young Christians. He exhorted them, which shows the earnestness of his appeal. He comforted them, which shows that he was not unmindful of their particularly trying circumstances and was as a result sensible in his exhortation. He charged them with firmness and without compromise. There was a tender definiteness in all his dealings with them.

c. The effect of Paul's life, 12. The effect of all this was that Paul's converts would also walk worthy of God. This is always the standard for all believers everywhere and in every age.

We need to be reminded before leaving this section of what Paul declared in verse 1 — the proof that his ministry at Thessalonica was not empty was the testimony of his converts. It was not a case of the preacher building himself up in the eyes of the people, but it was a case of the people gladly and fully affirming the effectiveness of the preacher's ministry among them. It is easy to do the former; it is rare to experience the latter. God give us more Christian workers in our day who will give themselves unselfishly and unstintingly to the work.

C. PAUL'S CONCERN FOR THE THESSALONIANS,
2:13 — 3:13

In this section we catch a glimpse of that which was Paul's concern for the church. It should be remembered how Paul and his companions were forced to leave the city before they had had much time to establish the young church. For this reason he had been anxious about the welfare of the group and had sent Timothy from Athens to ascertain their spiritual state. A good report came back and Paul was greatly encouraged. But in this section we discover what was on the apostle's heart, and it is plain that his concern was in the realm of spiritual things and not in the area of material lacks. And it is still true today that God's people should be concerned not about new facilities but chiefly about the spiritual state of the group.

1. *Concern About Sufferings,* 2:13 — 3:4

Paul first expresses the concern which he had lest the persecutions which the young church had to endure had shaken their faith. The report from Timothy had assured him that such was not the case and he gives thanks for that (v. 13). "For this cause" refers to what follows in the paragraph. The fact that they had not defected proves that the Thessalonians had received the preachers' message as the word of God. Paul's preaching was with conviction, for he believed that what he said was not of his own devising but was the word of God itself. Twice he employs the phrase in this single verse. The second occurrence is especially emphatic — "you accepted no word of men, but, as it truly is, God's word" (Findlay, *Cambridge Greek Testament,* p. 51). He also claims for the word effective, fructifying operation because it works (or is made to work, passive, as some think; Robinson, *Ephesians,* pp. 241-47) in the heart of the believer.

a.   The cause of their sufferings, 2:14-20. The result of their stand and activity for Christ was immediate persecution. The details are lacking, but the fact of it is clearly stated in Acts 17. The Gentile converts at Thessalonica had suffered from their fellow Gentiles (because the Jews in the city had aroused them by appealing to their political passions) just as the Christian Jews in Judea had suffered from their fellow Jews. Their cases were identical. The word *Jews* here is used in the sense of those who are the enemies of Christ (cf. II Cor. 11:24). They were one cause of suffering.

But the trouble was not only caused by men; God too had a purpose in it. This is seen in the phrase in verse 16, "to fill up their sins alway." Paul is saying that God allows His people to be persecuted sometimes in order to prove the evil nature of man and show the righteous character of His judgment when it comes (cf. Gen. 15:16; Dan. 8:23; Matt. 23:32). God allows the wicked to fill to the brim (the compound *anapleroo* implies a full measure) in order to demonstrate to all that His sure judgment is a righteous one. God's purpose is at work, too, in permitting suffering.

b.   The character of their sufferings, 2:14-20. In some cases the suffering was characterized by death itself (v. 15). This was true in the case of the prophets (like Stephen whom the Judean Jews killed) and of the Lord Himself (cf. Acts 4:27). At Thessalonica, however, things had not gone that far, and the sufferings of these believers took the form of persecution (v. 14). Paul himself had experienced more than his share of such as the Jews dogged his trail trying to forbid him to preach the gospel. The truth of verse 16 was illustrated in Paul's life at Antioch (Acts 13:45, 50), Iconium (Acts 14:1-5), Lystra (Acts 14:19), Berea (Acts 17:13), Corinth (Acts 18:12), and of course Thessalonica.

The suffering of these people was not characterized merely by persecution but by steadfastness in persecution. For this Paul expresses his ecstasy (vv. 17-20). This victory on the part of the believers was in spite of their being orphaned (this is the word translated "being taken from you" in v. 17) of their spiritual father, Paul. The expressions of bereavement in verse 17 which his departure caused, the repeated statements of attempts to go to them in verse 18, and the expressions of esteem in verse 19 all give the lie to any possible accusation which Paul's enemies may have brought against him that he quickly lost interest in his converts. They were to him his hope, joy, and crown of rejoicing at the coming of the Lord. Paul's exultation in the Thessalonians is so intense that the sentence is broken and difficult of punctuation (though the phrase *are not even ye* is best taken as a parenthesis in the sentence). It may be paraphrased thus: "What is our hope, or joy, or crown of rejoicing? Nothing, if you are not such in the presence of our Lord Jesus Christ at His coming. For truly you are our glory and joy."

c. The cure for their sufferings, 3:1-4. The chapter division is unfortunate here. The "wherefore" links this to the preceding section. Because of having to leave his converts, and because he had himself been hindered from returning to the

city, Paul sent Timothy back to see how the
young church was faring. He did this in spite of
the fact that it meant that he would have to be
left alone in Athens. Evidently Silas was still min-
istering in Berea and had not yet rejoined the
party. All three met again in Corinth where the
letter was written. As much as Paul loved the
Thessalonians, he hated to see Timothy leave him,
for he used a word that literally means "abandon"
(cf. Mark 12:19; Eph. 5:31). It is emphasized by
the word *alone* (v. 1) showing the sense of desola-
tion which overcame Paul in Athens as he faced
the philosophers of that city. Yes, even ministers
of the gospel feel depressed and alone at times.
However, it was important that Timothy go. He
is called by three terms of endearment — brother,
servant (cf. I Tim. 4:6 for the only other time
it is used of Timothy), and fellow worker (though
this is not in some texts). The word for "servant"
is not the word which means "slave," relating the
man to his work, but the word from which we get
the term *deacon,* relating the man to his work. It
is used here in the nontechnical sense of one who
renders service, and not in the technical sense of
deacon as a church officer. Timothy's service to
the Thessalonian church on this occasion was twofold. He was to establish them. The word contains
the idea of strengthening and is from a root which

means "a support." He was also to comfort them, but that word has more meaning than simply a neutral soothing of them in their difficulties. It also means encouraging or helping them positively for the battle that faced them.

Paul had reiterated to the Thessalonians when he was with them (the verb is imperfect in verse 4 and shows repeated telling) that persecution was to be expected. Therefore, he expected them to realize that the cure for sufferings was not relief from them, for no man was to be moved by them (v. 3). The word *moved* is used outside the New Testament of a dog wagging its tail and therefore comes to have the sense of "to fawn upon" or "to flatter." Thus Paul is saying that Timothy's job was to show the believers that they should not yield to flattery in the midst of testings. Undoubtedly some of the Jews were urging them to reject Christianity and turn to Judaism, but Paul was emphatically warning them that this would not cure their sufferings.

He further reminded them through Timothy that they should remember that affliction is the normal lot of a Christian and should not be regarded as something unusual or strange. We are appointed to such. "Appoint" is a strong word used, for instance, of a city set on a hill (Matt. 5:14) or of being set for the defense of the gospel

(Phil. 1:16). Sufferings are by divine appointment and the remembrance of this along with steadfastness is what is needed in the time of stress.

2. *Concern About Satan, 3:5*

Paul now reasserts his concern for the Christians as he did in verse 1. However, here there is greater emphasis on his personal concern for them as evidenced by the use of the singular in contrast to the plural in verse 1. His concern was for their faith that it was standing the test of time, in the midst of the temptations of Satan. Here the Devil is presented in his characteristic role of tempter (cf. Matt. 4:3; 6:13; Mark 1:13; I Cor. 7:5). The indicative mode which Paul used in the verb in the phrase *lest by some means the tempter have tempted you* shows that he was certain that the tempting had taken place — it "was already a fact" (Plummer, *A Commentary on St. Paul's First Epistle to the Thessalonians*, p. 47). However the use of the subjunctive mode in the phrase *and our labor be in vain* makes that a matter of doubt. In other words, he is sure that Satan has been tempting, but he does not think that the Thessalonians had been yielding. If they had, then his hard work would have indeed been in vain, but such he doubts to be the case.

3. *Concern About Shortcomings, 3:6-13*

a. The character of shortcomings, 6-10. When

Timothy returned from Thessalonica he brought with him a good report of the steadfastness of the believers (v. 6). This meant so much to Paul that he called it good news, literally "a gospel." It concerned the Thessalonians' faith (toward God) and love (toward man). Particularly, their love for Paul himself had not waned in his absence. That remembrance of him was good, that is, kindly or well-disposed; it was continuous — always; and it was reciprocal. Again we see Paul's tender love and concern for his converts. This good report brought comfort and life itself to Paul (vv.7-8). Their faith, love, and longing comforted the apostle. The word *comfort* means more than soothing; it means "strengthening," and it came to Paul at a time when he needed it, for he was in the midst of the pressure of affliction and distress. Both words imply trouble from without — "affliction" meaning "choking, pressing care," and "distress" signifying the crushing kind of trouble. It is easy to see why he speaks of his situation in such terms, for he was at Athens alone and had just suffered four successive experiences of apparent defeat since he set foot in Europe. At Philippi he had been cast in jail and asked to leave the city. At Thessalonica he had been forced to leave and to guarantee that he would not return. At Berea he was pursued by the Jews and compelled to move on.

At Athens he had had little success with the philosophers of the city. Surely he was in afflictions and distress and this news meant strength and life to him. It brought to him a revival of energy which was not a passing thing but a continual source of inspiration (note the present tense of the verb *we live* in verse 8). The construction of the clause *if ye stand fast in the Lord* is unusual, for the indicative is used, whereas this particular word for "if" usually takes the subjunctive. It "gives a touch of definiteness" (Morris, p. 67) and shows that Paul did not really have misgivings about their standing fast.

Because of this good report Paul expresses his thanksgiving for the Thessalonians (v. 9). Such thanksgiving is actually due God, for the compound verb *antapodounai,* render again, "shows that the thanksgiving is not really *giving* but *paying;* it is rendering what is *due*" (Plummer, p. 50). But, though Paul is grateful, he is not satisfied, for he continually made supplication (*deomenoi,* which is a stronger word than the simple *proseuchesthai,* pray) in order that he might see them again and have a part in their spiritual growth (v. 10). This prayer was intense, for Paul joins to the phrase *night and day* the adverb *exceedingly,* which is a very strong word and which is found in the New Testament elsewhere only in I Thessalonians 5:13 and Ephesians 3:20. This prayer was not answered until some years later (Acts 20:1-2), but Paul longed to perfect them. The word *perfect* means to render complete, as one might repair fishing nets (Matt. 4:21) or restore saints (Gal. 6:1; Eph. 4:12). The Thessalonians needed this ministry in order to supply that which was lacking in their faith. Paul did not consider that the great commission had been fulfilled when people were saved. He realized that there also had to be the work of building them up so that their faith would not be defective in any way. The great pastor's heart shows itself again in this verse.

b. The cure for shortcomings, 11:13. Paul now prays for the believers in order that they might be made complete in their faith. His first petition is that he might be brought to them. It would be God and Christ who would do this. It is important to notice that "our Lord Jesus Christ" is linked with "God himself" as closely as possible, and furthermore that the verb is singular. There could scarcely be a clearer way of emphasizing the deity of Christ and His equality with the Father. The verb *direct* means "make straight" as in Luke 1:79 and indicates a removing of the obstacles which Satan had put in Paul's way (cf. 2:18). The second petition is that the Thessalonians might abound in love toward one another and all men (v. 12). The

purpose of this is stated in verse 13. It is in order
that God might establish them in holiness. The
word *heart* indicates the whole personality as in
2:4 and James 5:8. The holiness spoken of here is
the resulting state of sanctification which is the
result of the process of sanctification. In the Septuagint it is used only of God and thus connotes a
high state. Abounding love would establish them
unblamable in the state of being set apart to God.
God Himself is the standard, and holiness is "before God." This idea is reinforced by mentioning
the appearance of Christ at His return with the
"holy ones." The phrase can mean "saints" who
accompany Christ as in 4:14 (Findlay, p. 76), or
it can mean "angels" as taught in Mark 8:38 (Plummer, p. 54), or it may include both, which is likely
here.

Throughout this section which has been dealing with causes for concern in the life of the
church we find indications of how to strengthen
the work in order that sufferings, Satan, or shortcomings will not hinder. For one thing, the work
of the ministers of Christ is an important factor
in keeping the church growing and healthy (2:17-
20; 3:2). This is exemplified by the ministries of
Paul and Timothy. For another thing, we see the
importance of prayer in the life and growth of the
church (3:11-13). Finally, we see the need for

knowledge of the truth of God in order to appraise correctly the events of life. This is exemplified in the matter of realizing that suffering is the appointed lot of the believer (3:3-4).

II

PRACTICAL AND HORTATORY
4:1 — 5:24

W E NOW PASS from the personal and historical
section of the letter to the practical and
hortatory part. This follows a normal pattern in
Paul's Epistles — doctrine, then duty; precept, then
practice. Paul has already rather incidentally mentioned the deficiencies in the lives of the Thessalonians and now he exhorts them to remedy these
shortcomings. The section is marked off by the
first two words, "furthermore then," which is an
expression indicating a new subject, not the close
of the letter (cf. Phil. 3:1).

A. CONCERNING DEVELOPMENT, 4:1-12

Before dealing with the specific things in which
the believers needed further development, Paul
opens this section with a word of general exhortation (vv. 1-2). He addresses them by the endearing
term *brethren*. Then he asks them to abound in
the things they knew. The verb *ask* is *erōtaō,* which

is generally used between those who are equal in rank, and again shows Paul's esteem for these people. It is the only word used by the Lord Jesus in His prayers to God (cf. John 14:16; 16:26; 17:9, 15, 20). This and I Thessalonians 5:12; II Thessalonians 2:1; and Philippians 4:3 are the only occurrences of the word in Paul's letters, and it is interesting to notice that they all occur in letters to Macedonian churches, as if to indicate that he held them in special esteem. Paul also exhorts them, but not with any superior air as the word *exhort* might imply, for his exhortation is "in the Lord." He reminds them that they had been told how they ought to walk and please God. The word *ought,* denotes *"moral necessity, lying in the relationship presupposed"* (Findlay, p. 81) (cf. II Thess. 3:7; Rom. 1:27; etc.). Pleasing God is not a matter of choice for the Christian, it is a necessity which grows out of his relationship to Christ. Furthermore, pleasing God (cf. I Thess. 2:4; Rom. 2:29; 8:8; I Cor. 4:5; 7:32 ff.; Gal. 1:10; II Tim. 2:4; Heb. 11:5-6) is something which is never final in this life, for we must continually be abounding in it. The Christian life should be marked by constant growth. Paul reminds them what commandments he had given them. The word translated "commandments" is not a common one in the New Testament and signifies instruction which is given by a superior to a subordinate. It is often used of military orders. But these were no arbitrary commands of the apostle; they were given through the Lord Jesus, and that is why he can exhort the believers to abound in them.

1. *Abound in Abstinence,* 4:1-8

After this word of introduction Paul deals with the first specific lack in the lives of the Thessalonians. It should be remembered that heathen life in those days was characterized by general sexual laxity. Ritual fornication played a large place in the heathen religious worship rites, and moral looseness was common among people on all levels of society. Since this was the environment in which the Thessalonians had been reared, it is easy to see why they did not have strong convictions and high standards on this subject. Nevertheless, Christianity does not take its standards from the society in which it is planted; it receives them from God Himself. Therefore, Paul deals with this matter of fornication in no uncertain terms.

He begins by putting the whole subject on the highest plane — "this is the will of God, even your sanctification, that ye should abstain from fornication" (v. 3). God's will includes sanctification, and since sanctification includes holiness in body as well as spirit (cf. I Thess. 5:23) fornication nullifies it. To sanctify means to set apart for God or to be holy. Since every believer is already sanctified in Christ (I Cor. 6:11; Heb. 10:10), a common New Testament designation of all believers is "saints," or holy ones (cf. 3:13). "Thus sainthood, or sanctification, is not an attainment, it is the state into which God, in grace, calls sinful men, and in which they begin their course as Christians" (Hogg and Vine, *The Epistles of Paul the Apostle to the Thessalonians,* p. 114). Sanctification is also used in the Scriptures of the goal of life which every believer should be pursuing (Heb. 12:14), and that involves separation from evil things and in particular from fornication. Verse 3 states the requirement negatively ("from fornication"). Verse 4 states it positively. However, there is debate over the meaning of "vessel." Some think it means "body" and that Paul is saying that the believer is to gain the mastery over his body in order to keep himself pure in matters of sex. If this be the meaning the idea is similar to that of I Corinthians 9:24-27, and the use of the word *vessel* is somewhat parallel to II Corinthians 4:7. Others think the word *vessel* means "wife" as in I Peter 3:7 and that the verb *possess* indicates courtship and contracting of marriage. In this case Paul is expressing an idea similar to that in I Corinthians 7:2, and verse 4 here describes the honorable entry into matrimony, while verse 5 concerns the proper maintenance of that estate. In either case, that is, whether Paul is referring to the chastity of one's own body or the relation with one's own wife, he declares that it should not be in lust as is the case with the Gentiles. Even in a marriage dominated by lust there can be no honor or sanctity in the union. The word *lust* "signifies not, like Eng. 'passion,' a violent feeling, but an overmastering feeling, in which the man is borne along by evil as though its passive instrument" (Findlay, p. 86). This was true of the Gentile neighbors of these believers, and it was true because they "knew not God"; i.e., they had rejected the light which God had given them (cf. Romans 1:21,28).

Verse 6 is probably to be understood as the result of obedience to the injunctions of verses 3 and 4. If fornication is abstained from, no man will go beyond his brother. "Go beyond" means "to transgress" or "overreach," while "defraud" has the idea of taking advantage and implies avarice and covetousness. A sexual sin is a fraud against a brother because it takes what is rightly his. Paul uses "brother" here not in the restricted sense of a brother in Christ but in the general sense of a brother man. There is no other instance in Paul's writings of this use of brother. Paul reminds his readers that unbecoming conduct will not go unpunished, "for the Lord is the avenger of all such."

Another reason for heeding the exhortation of verses 3 through 6 is stated in verses 7 and 8. The Christian should maintain purity of life not only from fear that God will judge (v. 6b) but also because of the grandeur of his calling in Christ to holiness. There are two different prepositions used in verse 7. God has not called unto (with a view to) uncleanness. The idea is purpose. Rather He has called us in holiness. Sanctification as used in this passage, then, is not the ultimate aim, nor the gradual attainment of the Christian life, but it is the ruling condition and atmosphere in which the believer lives. Since this is so, therefore (v. 8 is a conclusion), to despise this truth is to despise God. To treat lightly the commands of the apostle with regard to sexual purity (v. 2) is to attempt to treat lightly the One who cannot be disregarded. Thus, behind the commandments of the missionaries lie the immutable laws of God Himself. And it is this God who has made victory possible for the believer by giving the Holy Spirit. The participle *give* is in the present tense not because God repeatedly gives the Holy Spirit but because the participial form is used to describe God, as in 1:10 where Jesus is called the deliverer. The Spirit was given at the time of salvation (Rom. 8:9), and He is the available inner power for victory (cf. I Cor. 6:19). "The way to escape the Avenger is to fly to the Giver and accept and cherish His gift" (Plummer, p. 64).

2. *Abound in Affection,* 4:9-10.

Christianity should always be distinguished by purity and love. This latter is the next thing in which Paul asks the Thessalonians to abound.

a. The explanation of love. Paul speaks in these verses not of love in general but of brotherly love (*philadelphia*). This means the love that particularly binds together the children of one father. Love is the seeking of the highest good in the one loved, and the highest good is the glory or manifestation of God. Therefore, brotherly love is that special desire to seek the glory of God in the lives of other members of the household of faith. This is something which Paul says he need not write about for God Himself teaches it. The reference is not to some external revelation from God but to the work of God in the believer's heart teaching him to love. It is strikingly related to the reference to the Holy Spirit in the preceding verse (see also Rom. 5:5).

b. The extent of love. This kind of love is to extend to all the brethren (v. 10). The extent of love should be limited only by the opportunities afforded to express it.

c.   The expression of love. Paul probably has in the back of his mind here the way the Thessalonians expressed their love for their brethren by providing hospitality. This is one of the principal means of showing love (cf. Rom. 12:13; I Tim. 3:2; Titus 1:8; Heb. 13:1-2; I Peter 4:9), and since Thessalonica was the commercial center of Macedonia, the believers there had undoubtedly many occasions to play host to Christians from other places.

d.   The expansion of love. Paul urges the increase of such love, for in brotherly love there is always room for growth.

3.   *Abound in Ambition,* 4:11-12

Following this admonition concerning love, Paul now urges his readers to have certain ambitions. First he exhorts them to be ambitious to be distinguished in being quiet. The word *be ambitious* is used elsewhere only in Romans 15:20 and II Corinthians 5:9. Quiet is the opposite of restlessness (as Luke 14:4; 23:56; Acts 11:18). It means tranquility of mind, and this comes only when one's whole desire in life is to let Christ be magnified in his life. When selfish ambitions are the governing principles of life there can only be unrest, but when Christ completely controls there will be rest and the fulfillment of this admonition to be ambitious to have no ambition of one's own! Such an attitude (ambition) will also involve two things: tending to one's own affairs, and working with one's own hands. There is evidence that some of these believers were restless because they believed that there was no need to work since the Lord would come very soon. Therefore, they may have been sponging off the other Christians in the church. Paul undoubtedly had these people in mind when giving these injunctions. The great purpose of a dedicated life that tends to its own business is to have an honest testimony toward the unsaved world. "Honestly" means "becomingly" or "decently," and the thought is related in this verse to those outside Christianity. In one sense believers are to live without regard to the standards of the world, and in another sense the opposite is true. Here Paul is urging the Thessalonians so to live that the unbelievers may see in their lives the difference between order and confusion, idleness and diligence, sponging and independence. Such a life will be independent of the help of others, and this is the meaning of the last phrase in verse 12. Maintain an honorable independence and thus maintain a decent testimony to unbelievers.

B. Concerning the Dead, 4:13-18

As has been suggested, the cause of restlessness among some of the Thessalonian Christians was the belief that since the Lord's coming was imminent there was no point in working any longer. The entire subject of the return of Christ had thus come to the Apostle's mind. It is clear that Paul had taught much about this subject while he was in the city (II Thess. 2:5), but the main point of his teaching had evidently concerned the advent of Christ and not the resurrection. In the meantime perhaps some of the believers had died, and the question arose, "Had their premature deaths caused them to lose all hope of sharing in the glorious reign of Christ?" The fact that this question did arise points to the early date of the Epistle, for only at the very beginning of the church when but a few had had time to die could it have caused such great anxiety (Salmon, *Introduction to the New Testament,* p. 363). That this agitation had arisen over this matter was probably reported to Paul by Timothy on his return from the city. Paul's answer to the problem is a reassuring affirmation that the dead will be raised and will therefore share in the kingdom.

1. *We Have a Preview,* 4:13-14

The certainty of the Christian's resurrection is based on the fact of Christ's resurrection. The

formula *I would not have you to be ignorant* is
found frequently in Paul's writings when he wishes
to explain some new point (cf. Rom. 1:13; 11:25;
I Cor. 10:1; 12:1; II Cor. 1:8). The subject is
"those who sleep." The present participle is used
(signifying continuousness) and can either mean
"those that are lying asleep" or "those who fall
asleep from time to time." The verb *to sleep* is
used of natural sleep (Matt. 28:13; Acts 12:6; etc.)
and of death, but only the death of a Christian
(as here and I Cor. 7:39; II Pet. 3:4; etc.). The
word is particularly suggestive when used in the
latter sense. "The object of the metaphor is to
suggest that as the sleeper does not cease to exist
while his body sleeps, so the dead person continues to exist despite his absence from the region
in which those who remain can communicate with
him, and that, as sleep is known to be temporary,
so the death of the body will be found to be.
Sleep has its waking, death will have its resurrection" (Hogg and Vine, p. 128). Because of this,
any sorrow which the Christian may have over
the loss of a loved one (and it is comforting to
remember that our Lord wept when his friend
Lazarus died, John 11:33-35) is unlike the hopeless despair which the heathen can only have. But
Paul is not really saying that Chritsians may sorrow but not to the same degree as the heathen,

for that meaning would strain the "even as." He is saying that Christians are not *like* the heathen because Christians do not sorrow. He does not necessarily deny that we may grieve over loss (cf. Phil. 2:27), but that is not the point here. Sorrow characterizes the heathen and therefore cannot characterize the Christian. "Against this deep sorrow of the world the word *sleep,* four times applied in this context to the Christian's death, is an abiding protest" (Findlay, p. 96).

This certainty is based on the preview seen in the resurrection of Christ. The "if" clause is a first class condition and assumes the fact. Therefore it may be translated "since we believe." The condition being true, the result is also true; i.e., God will bring with Christ into His kingdom those who have fallen asleep through Jesus. The last phrase, *through Jesus,* is related to the fact that death has been changed to sleep through the work of Jesus. Heathen hopelessness in the face of death is seen in the following quotation from a letter of the second century: "Eirene to Taonnophris and Philon, good cheer! I was as much grieved and shed as many tears over Eumoiros as I shed for Didymas, and I did everything that was fitting, and so did my whole family, . . . But still there is nothing one can do in the face of such trouble. So I leave you to comfort yourselves. Good-bye"

(Deissmann, *New Light on the New Testament,*
p. 76).

2. *We Have a Promise,* 4:15

Next comes the positive declaration that the
Christian dead will actually be raised first and
will therefore undoubtedly have a share in the
kingdom. The statement is made as authoritative
as possible by stating that it is the word of the
Lord. There are two possible explanations of this.
It could be an otherwise unrecorded saying of
Christ (cf. Acts 20:35) or it may have come to
Paul by direct revelation (cf. Acts 16:6; 18:9).
In any case, the Thessalonians need not be wor-
ried; in reality the dead will have a foremost place,
for the living shall in no wise (emphatic negative)
precede those who are asleep at the Lord's return.
Notice that Paul included himself among that living group and evidently expected to live until
the return of Christ (cf. Phil. 4:5; Titus 2:13;
written later in his life). One of the wonderful
things about the hope of His coming is that it
burns brightly in the hearts of each generation of
Christians regardless of how long His return is
delayed.

3. *We Have a Picture,* 4:16-18

Paul now fills in the details of the picture of
what will happen when the Lord returns.

a. **A return, 16. Christ Himself will return.**

The word *Himself* is in the emphatic position in
the sentence and emphasizes that no intermediary,
but the Lord Himself, will usher in this great
event. Because it will be He Himself who comes,
the attendant circumstances will display all the
grandeur due His personal presence. There will
be a shout. It is a word of command used in
classical Greek for the shout with which an officer gives the order to his troops or his crew. There *PAROUSIA*
is in the word a ring of authority and a note of
urgency. It is not said who utters the shout, whether
it is the Lord or an archangel. However, the voice
of an archangel will be heard. Michael is the only
archangel mentioned in the Bible (Jude 9), but it
is not impossible that there are other archangels
(notice the absence of the definite article here —
an archangel, not the archangel). Though Gabriel
is mentioned as a high-ranking angel (Dan. 8:16;
9:21; Luke 1:19, 26) he is not specifically designated as an archangel. The Jews listed seven chief
angels together. The trumpet of God will also
sound when He comes. This is also referred to
twice in I Corinthians 15:52.

b. A resurrection, 16. Again the priority of
the dead is mentioned, for they shall be raised
first. It is not that they shall be raised before the
rest of the dead but before those who are alive
at the Lord's coming are changed. "Dead in

Christ" is of course an alternative description of those who "sleep in Jesus."

c. A rapture, 17. Next in order ("then," *epeita*, implies order of events and not necessarily any lengthy interval between) there will be the change in the living. We shall be caught up. The word means "seize" or "snatch" and the Latin translation of this verb uses the word from which we get "rapture" in English. Thus the translation of living believers is called the rapture of the church. Rapture means the act of conveying a person from one place to another and thus is properly used of this transport of the living to heaven. Paul used it of his own experience of being caught up into the third heaven (II Cor. 12:2, 4; cf. also Rev. 12:5). It would appear from these other occurences of the word that Paul had in mind being taken into heaven and not just into the mid-air to turn around suddenly and return to the earth. He also implies in this idea of rapture the necessary change in mortal bodies in order to fit them for immortal existence in heaven. This is stated in greater detail in I Corinthians 15:50-53, and while the method of this change is never revealed, it is clear that Paul believed that it is possible to have a metamorphosis without the dissolution caused by death.

d. A reunion, 17. The reunion is actually twofold. It is first of all with loved ones who have died, for we shall be caught up together with them. Second, it is a meeting with the Lord in the air (with a view to proceeding on into heaven, not returning to the earth immediately, as stated above). "The natural consequence of this blissful meeting with the Lord is that there will be no subsequent parting" (Plummer, p. 77). After His return there will be uninterrupted union and communion with our Lord.

e. A reassurance, 18. As a result of what has been stated there should be no sorrowing but rather comfort concerning those who have died. Notice how Paul sticks to the subject — the dead in Christ. He says nothing in this passage about the resurrection of the wicked, the intermediate state, judgment, means of translation, or reign with Christ. In this passage our hope is centered on the assurance of the resurrection of the dead in Christ, the change in the living, and the eternal union with our Lord. Repeating these truths will bring assurance to the heart.

C. Concerning the Day of the Lord, 5:1-11

A second difficulty in relation to the return of Christ comes up for discussion. Not only were the believers concerned about the fate of loved ones who died before the return, but like so many others they wanted to know something about *when* the event would occur. The disciples also had asked when (Mark 13:3-4), and the Lord had told them that He could not give them any new light on the question (Acts 1:7). Paul, too, appeals to what they already know and asks them to wait patiently and work hard in the meantime. We need not think that the question was prompted by idle curiosity. If the time of the appearing is unknown, it is natural to be apprehensive about whether anyone now alive will live to see it. Paul tries to show his readers that certain things about the coming of the Lord are more important than whether they would be alive when it occurred.

1. *The Meaning of the Day of the Lord,* 5:1-2

The Day of the Lord was the subject of much Old Testament revelation. Many passages speak of it either under that full designation or under the shorter phrase *that day* (cf. Isa. 2:12; 4; 13:9-11; Joel 1:15 ff.; Amos 5:18; Zeph. 1:14-16; 3:14 ff.). A study of these and other passages will show that the Day of the Lord is a time of judgment and blessing. It is a time when God deals with the world in judgment for its sin; it is the period of great tribulation on the earth. But it is also a time of blessing when the earth shall enjoy the personal reign of Christ during the millennium. Thus the Day of the Lord as revealed in the Old Testament includes first a time of wrath and judgment on the wicked, followed by the era of peace when Christ will rule over the earth.

However, in this passage Paul is not discussing the entire Day of the Lord but only its coming. This is important, for it explains why he deals only with the judgment aspect of that day. Also, this is something which was known to them both from the Old Testament and from Paul's own teaching (cf. II Thess. 2:4). Note that the first word of the verse indicates a contrast, "but." This shows that the subject preceding, i.e., the rapture of the living and the resurrection of the dead in Christ, was not the subject of Old Testament revelation nor of Paul's teaching while with them. Paul affirms this in I Corinthians 15:51 when he calls this same subject a mystery; i.e., something unrevealed in the Old Testament. The very fact that these Christians did not know about the rapture and resurrection of believers accounts for their perplexity about it. *But* of the Day of the Lord they should have known perfectly well. They became confused about it later (as seen from II Thess. 2), but it could not be blamed on the fact that they could not know either from the Old Testament or from a careful listening to Paul's teaching. In particular they knew about the times (the duration) and the seasons (the characteristics) of the Day of the Lord. That means they knew something about duration and characteristics particularly as they related to the coming of the Day of the Lord. It would be as a thief in the night. "The unexpectedness of the coming of the thief, and the unpreparedness of those to whom he comes, are the essential elements in this figure" (Hogg and Vine, p. 154). The same simile was used by Christ in Matthew 24:43 and Relevation 3:3.

2.	*The Method of the Day of the Lord, 5:3*

The Day of the Lord will delude and destroy. It will delude because men will be saying (the verb is in the continuous present tense) "peace and safety" when the day overtakes them. At the very moment when the world feels secure (this is the meaning of the rather rare word translated "safety," cf. Luke 1:4; Acts 5:23 for its only other occurrences) and people are assuring themselves and each other that all is well, sudden destruction will come on them. Destruction is not annihilation but "utter and hopeless *ruin,* the loss of all that gives worth to existence" (Milligan, p. 65). This is compared with birth pangs, a familiar simile in the Scriptures (Isa. 13:6-8; 37:3; Hos. 13:13; Mic. 4:9; Mark 13:8), and the comparison involves inevitable certainty, suddenness, and intense pain. The certainty is particularly emphasized in this passage by the last clause, "they shall not escape." There are several similarities of language in this verse with Luke 21:34, a fact which is not surprising in light of the friendship between Paul and Luke.

3. *The Message of the Day of the Lord,* 5:4-11

Truth is always practical, and the doctrine of the Day of the Lord and particularly its sudden coming is intensely so.

a. It examines, 4-5. The coming of the Day of the Lord will be a great divider between children of light and children of darkness. Thus it behooves one to examine himself and be sure to which group he belongs. Paul expresses his confidence that the Thessalonians were children of light with a strong "but you." Negatively, they were not children of darkness (v. 4), and positively they were children of the day (v. 5). The reference to day in verse 5 is not to the Day of the Lord mentioned earlier but to "day" as a synonym for light and as the opposite of darkness or night.

b. It exhorts, 6-8. Actually the exhortation begins with the last part of verse 5 where Paul changes from "ye" to "we," associating himself with those who need to observe the injunctions which follow. There are two: watch and be sober. Watching involves alertness. In other passages it is accompanied by prayer (Mark 13:33-34; Col. 4:2). It is the opposite of indifference, which is the idea of the word *sleep* in verse 6. This is a different word for sleep from that used in 4:13 ff. and is regularly used of moral indifference (cf. Mark 13:36; Eph. 5:14). It is aptly characteristic of those who morally are of the night. Whereas watching is more mental, sobriety is more moral. It excludes actual drunkenness (Luke 12:45; though there is no inference that these people were given to that) and self-indulgence (I Tim. 3:2; Titus 2:2) and emphasizes the need for stability and balance in view of the Lord's return. Be alert and be stable is what Paul is enjoining.

These exhortations of verse 6 are reinforced in verse 7 by reminding the readers that those who are of the night do the very opposite. They sleep and are drunk. This is to be understood in its natural sense and as a statement of the facts of life. But the natural is used in an analogy with the spiritual. As sleep is natural in the night, so indifference to God is natural for the unredeemed man. As drunkenness is natural at night, so instability is natural to the unregenerate man. But the redeemed are not of the night; therefore, let us be alert and be stable.

The Christian's sobriety evidently brought to Paul's mind the picture of a soldier on duty, and therefore he mentions the believer's armor (v. 8; cf. Rom. 13:12; Eph. 6:11-17). The tenses in Greek are revealing. "Be sober" is present tense, indicating that this should be the continual attitude of the Christian, while "putting on" is aorist, which expresses momentary action. If the putting on were present tense it would imply that the Christian might at some time or other lay aside his armor, which is unthinkable. The aorist says, "Put your armor on and leave it on." It is a once-for-all step. The breastplate consists of faith and love, and the helmet is the hope of salvation. Here once again we see the triad of Christian graces — faith, hope, and love. While the details of the particular pieces of armor differ in the different passages where the figure is used, in no passage is a piece covering the back mentioned, for the Christian once engaged in the fight does not turn in flight.

c. It encourages, 9-11. The hope of salvation which is the helmet mentioned in the previous verse means the full realization of our salvation in the future. The assurance of this hope being fulfilled is the fact that God has appointed us not to wrath but to salvation. "Appointed" is not so strong as "predestined" (as in Rom. 8:29), but it does place the initiative and responsibility on God for our salvation. The wrath is the anguish and tribulation associated with the beginning of the Day of the Lord (v. 3), and it is from this that the believer has been delivered by the "de-

liverer from the wrath to come" (1:10). Instead
we are to obtain salvation and this has been effected through the Lord Jesus Christ and based
on His death (v. 10). His death also effected
our union with Him, which in turn affects our
total existence so that whether we are awake (alive
on earth) or asleep (dead as far the body is concerned) we are still with Him. This is the source
of comfort and the substance of edification (v. 11).

The fact that in verse 10 is the only mention of
the death of Christ in this his earliest Epistle does
not mean that Paul was still developing his theology. He had been saved for nearly a score of
years and had been actively in the Lord's work
for almost a decade before this letter was written.
The subject matter of the letter concerned other
topics, and in reality the very fact that he mentions the death of Christ at all in the midst of other
discussions shows how firmly it was a part of his
doctrine. It is also interesting to notice the brief
mention here of the doctrine of union with Chri..
which Paul expounds elaborately in other Epistles.
Since this is not the subject here either, it shows
that this major doctrine was already firmly fixed
in Paul's mind and theology.

D.   CONCERNING DUTIES, 5:12-24

This practical section of the Epistle, which began

at 4:1, draws to a close with certain miscellaneous instructions to the church.

1. *In Relation to Saints and Society*, 5:12-15

a. Rules for the governed, 12-13. Paul begins with a word of regulation concerning the government of the church. There were two unusual situations among this group which made this admonition necessary. First of all, there was the problem caused by those who had stopped working because of their belief in the nearness of the second coming. Undoubtedly the leaders had rebuked them and the rebuke had not been well received. Therefore, Paul enjoins them to listen to the rulers of the church. Second, all the members of this church were new Christians, and most of them had been converted about the same time. Some, however, had become officers in the church. It was difficult for a few to take orders from those whom they had known all their lives and who had been saved about the same time. While it is true that in the church all have equal spiritual privileges and blessings, it is not true that all have equal office, for there are differences of gifts, and among these gifts is the gift of government (I Cor. 12:28). If there are those who govern there are those who are governed. To this latter group Paul says three things: know the leaders, esteem them, and be at peace. To know in the fullest sense means to know in their true character and to appreciate. To esteem (v. 13) is to think highly of the leaders. To be at peace means no schism, and this injunction is broadened to include all.

b. Rules for the governors, 12. In turn, we see in these admonitions something of what the duties of the leaders were. Paul mentions three things: they labor, they preside, and they admonish the people. It is clear that these are the duties of the same persons because of the single article before the three participles which describe their work. It is not too early in the history of the church to have had officers, for Paul appointed elders as early as the return from the first missionary journey (Acts 14:23). In general, these elders were to labor (this is the same word as appears in noun form in 1:3). It means that kind of work which causes one to grow weary in the doing of it — to toil with effort is the idea. It is a favorite word of Paul's used frequently to describe the arduous character of his own ministry (cf. I Cor. 15:10; Gal. 4:11; Phil. 2:16; Col. 1:29; I Tim. 4:10). In particular the leaders were over the people; that is, they presided over the affairs of the church. This verb *preside* is found elsewhere in the New Testament in Romans 12:8; I Timothy 3:4, 5, 12; 5:17; and Titus 3:8. To preside is not to dictate, and yet it is to lead, for even in an ordinary meeting the presiding officer has a certain amount of control by virtue of his position. Too, these officers were to admonish the people. The word means literally "to put in mind" and "has apparently always a sense of *blame* attached to it" (Milligan, p. 72). That is why this same word is translated "warn" in verse 14. It is because of the faithful carrying forward of the work on the part of the leaders that they are to be highly thought of (v. 13). Leaders' reputations should arise from the quality of their work and not from any other cause.

c. Rules for the group, 14-15. The words of verse 14 are not specifically addressed to the leaders and show that certain duties are the responsibility of the entire congregation. However, because of what has just been said, they have some special reference to the officers if only that they are to take the lead in carrying them out. There are four specific things to be done. First, warn the unruly. For the meaning of "warn" see the previous discussion on "admonish." The word *unruly* is a military term signifying the soldier who does not keep in proper rank. Thus it comes to mean anything out of order and may in this present passage have special reference to idleness and neglect of duties (cf. Milligan, p. 73). Second, comfort the feeble-minded. "Feeble-minded" is not a good rendering of a word which literally means "little-souled" or "faint-hearted." Perhaps the reference in this context is to those who were discouraged because some of their loved ones had died before the appearing of the Lord, and they needed encouragement. Third, support the weak. The reference is to those who were weak spiritually. Symptoms of spiritual weakness could be instability, inability to face persecution, yielding to the attacks of Satan, all of which may have been present in the Thessalonian church. "These, and all such as these, are to be the peculiar objects of the shepherd's care, since, more than the rest, they need the sympathy and help of those who are of maturer Christian experience" (Hogg and Vine, p. 183). Fourth, be patient toward all men. The word *be patient* literally means "be long-tempered" and is the exact opposite of "be short-tempered." The corresponding noun is regularly translated "longsuffering." This is to be the characteristic of the Christian in relation to all men.

In addition to these four specific duties of the group, there are two general admonitions given in verse 15. The first is a negative injunction — do not render evil for evil. This prohibition of retaliation is found also in Romans 12:17 and I Peter 3:9. It was particularly apropos in the case of the Thessalonian Christians, who were faced with

persecution, and it must have been difficult not
to want to retaliate under those pressures. But
Paul does not hesitate to put the matter plainly
to them. The negative is followed by a positive
statement, "follow that which is good." The good
is that which is especially helpful to others — the
beneficial. This is to be the rule of life always
and to all men.

2. *In Relation to Self,* 5:16-24

Paul now turns to matters which concern the
individual more particularly than the group,
though it is always true that the group is no
stronger than the individuals that make it up.
The former section dealt with what might be
termed external duties, while the present one
concerns the exercise of internal piety.

a. Be happy, 16. The command to rejoice ever-
more is somewhat startling in a letter written to
a suffering people. It must have struck the readers
as something of a paradox, and yet Paul had learned
the secret of true joy. It must not depend on circumstances, for in the world the Christian will
have tribulation (John 16:33). The ground for
lasting joy is found in eternal things, in the Lord
(Phil. 3:1), in the gospel (Acts 13:48; John 4:36),
and in seeing fellow believers grow in the truth
(III John 4). Incidentally, this verse, not John

11:35, is the shortest verse in the Greek New Testament.

b. Be prayerful, 17. The Christian's joy puts him in the proper mood to pray without ceasing. Paul has already used the word *without ceasing* twice of his own remembrance of the Thessalonians (1:3; 2:13) and now he enjoins it on the believers. Outside the New Testament the word is used of a hacking cough and aptly illustrates what Paul has in mind here about prayer. Just as a person with a hacking cough is not always audibly coughing though the tendency to cough is always there, so the Christian who prays without ceasing is not always praying audibly and yet prayer is always the attitude of his heart and life.

c. Be thankful, 18. This trilogy of injunctions concludes with the exhortation to be thankful in every circumstance (cf. Eph. 5:20; Phil. 4:6; Col. 3:17). The meaning is not that we are to be thankful *for* everything, but *in* the midst of any situation or circumstance we should find causes for thanksgiving in what God has done for us. This triad of precepts is without question the will of God for the believer.

d. Be discerning, 19-21. These three verses have to do with the work of the Holy Spirit in the individual and in the assembly. Verse 19 condemns quenching the spirit. The word is used of putting out a fire (Mark 9:48; Heb. 11:34) and is appropriately used in relation to the Spirit (cf. Matt. 3:11; Acts 2:3). The tense is present, and since this is a command, it means "stop quenching the Spirit"; that is, stop doing something you are now doing, not merely beware of doing it at some future time. Evidently the situation at Thessalonica was the opposite from that in Corinth where Paul later had to warn the church against disorderliness in relation to the gifts of the Spirit. At Thessalonica some were frowning on any manifestation of the Spirit that was at all out of the ordinary. This might be expected from the Macedonians who were more advanced culturally than those who lived in the south of Greece. They would be more prone to want to stifle the exercise of the unusual gifts of the Spirit.

In particular (v. 20) these believers are warned against despising prophesying. To despise is to make utterly nothing of, or to reduce to nothing, and this is what some were apparently doing in relation to prophecy. There are two aspects to prophesying, forthtelling (and at Thessalonica this may have included admonitions to the believers because of their idleness) and foretelling (and this may have involved messages concerning the second advent).

However, Paul does not advocate an uncritical acceptance of everything that claims to be of the Spirit. He requires the proving or testing of all things (v. 21; cf. I Cor. 12:3). That which is found to be good (the word means "genuine" in contrast to the counterfeit) should be heeded. "The chaff must be sifted from the wheat" (Findlay, p. 129).

e. Be particular, 22. Verse 22 states the negative of verse 21 and broadens the principle to include all areas of life. Every appearance or visible form of evil is to be avoided by the Christian. The word *form* could indicate every kind of evil, but the uniform New Testament usage favors the idea "every visible form or outward show of evil" (Luke 3:22; 9:29; John 5:37; II Cor. 5:7). Different kinds of evil is a quasi-philosophical idea, but it is a concrete truth that evil appears in many different forms.

f. Be holy, 22-24. Finally, Paul exhorts his beloved readers to complete holiness (v. 23) on the basis of the assured help of God (v. 24). The word *wholly* is found only here in the New Testament and is made up of two words, "complete" and "end." Thus the ideas of wholeness and completion are included. This is entire sanctification, and it is the work of God. It is further explained by the prayer that the whole spirit, soul, and body be preserved blameless. Some take this verse to prove the threefold nature of man (called trichoto-my), but it is not best taken as a proof text for this.[1] Paul is not analyzing man here (such an analysis would have to include "heart" and "mind") but is praying for complete sanctification in aim and in extent, and it is the faithfulness of God which assures the answer to the prayer.

Conclusion, 5:25-28. In the conclusion Paul makes a request, sends greetings, instructions, and a benediction. The request is a simple one for prayer for himself. It shows something of how very human Paul was. Similar requests are found in II Thessalonians 3:1 ff.; Romans 15:30; Ephesians 6:19; and Colossians 4:3 ff. The greetings were sent in the familiar form of the holy kiss. Not too much is known of the custom except that it seemed to be the practice of the early church to greet one another on the Lord's day with a kiss on the cheek, the men kissing other men and the women other women. Like many things it be-came abused in due time and had to be restricted because of the poor testimony to the heathen. The instruction to read the Epistle is put in very strong language (v. 27). The word *charge* really means "to bind with an oath." He wanted to be certain that what he had said was heard by every-

---

[1]For a recent treatment of this problem, see W. David Stacey, *The Pauline View of Man* (London: Macmillan & Co., Ltd., 1956), pp. 123-127.

one. Finally, the Epistle concludes with a prayer for grace for his readers, whom he loved so dearly in the Lord.

SECOND THESSALONIANS

1. *His revelation,* 2:3b
2. *His religion,* 2:4-5
3. *His power,* 2:9-10
4. *His punishment,* 2:8

D. RELATION OF THE DAY OF THE LORD TO THE RESTRAINER, 2:6-7

E. RELATION OF THE DAY OF THE LORD TO UNBELIEVERS, 2:10-12

F. RELATION OF THE DAY OF THE LORD TO THE BELIEVER, 2:13-17
   1. *The believer's position,* 2:13-14
   2. *The believer's practice,* 2:15-17

III. CORRECTION CONCERNING PRACTICE, 3:1-15

A. THE DISORDERLY ONES, 3:6-13
   1. *The penalty for the disorderly,* 3:6
   2. *The pattern for the disorderly,* 3:7-9
   3. *The precept for the disorderly,* 3:10
   4. *The pursuits for the disorderly,* 3:11-13

B. THE DISOBEDIENT ONES, 3:14-15

Conclusion, 3:16-18

THE SALUTATION

S ECOND THESSALONIANS was written shortly after
the first Epistle and with a background of fresh
information concerning the state of the church.
Whoever delivered the first letter to the church
had evidently brought back word concerning con-
ditions, and this second letter was written in light
of this report. It is primarily a letter of correction
— correction concerning persecution (chapter 1),
concerning prophecy (chapter 2), and concerning
practice (chapter 3).

The salutation of this Epistle is longer than that
of the first one. It begins in the customary manner; that is, with the name of the writer followed
by that of the recipient. Again Silas and Timothy
are linked with Paul not because they were co-
authors of the letter but because they had shared
the ministry in the city. The church, too, is
addressed in the same way as in the first letter —
"the church of the Thessalonians" — and it is a way
that is different from the designations in the other

Pauline Epistles. The only difference between the first verses of the two Epistles is the addition of the word *our* in this one. Here it points out God's fatherhood over believers instead of His relation as Father to Christ His Son. Although the church found herself in the place of persecution, her position was in God our Father and the Lord Jesus Christ.

The second verse adds the words *from God our Father and the Lord Jesus Christ,* which are probably not genuine in the same verse of the first letter. They remind us that the source of grace and peace is in God and Christ. In these simple words, *grace* and *peace,* are encompassed God's answer to all of man's need, for grace is that which provides the source of all spiritual blessings and particularly the blessing of salvation through Christ, and peace, that wholeness which grace brings.

I

CORRECTION CONCERNING
PERSECUTION
1:3-12

PERSECUTION SEEMED TO BE the peculiar lot of the church at Thessalonica. It was born in persecution (Acts 17:1-9) and grew in spite of continued tribulation (I Thess. 1:6; 2:14; 3:1-3). Some of the believers, however, seemed to be asking the question, Why? To do so was only natural, so in this chapter Paul gives them a prescription for persecution, and like all good prescriptions it was a combination of several ingredients.

A. IN PERSECUTION HAVE YOUR HEART RIGHT,
1:3-4

Because of the steadfastness of the people under trial Paul seized every occasion to praise them, and he does so again in verse 3. "We are bound to thank God" appears stiff at first glance, but it indicates that some of the believers had disclaimed the praise that Paul gave them in the first letter; so by using the words *we are bound* he shows that the circumstances of their spiritual condition compelled him to praise them. The thought is taken further in the phrase *as it is meet*, which indicates that the praise which Paul was showering on them was no more than they deserved.

What was it in the lives of the Thessalonians that called forth such commendation from the great apostle? It was two things, and these make up the prescription for the heart in times of persecution. First of all, their faith continued to grow. Earlier Paul had been anxious about the faith of his converts (I Thess. 3:2,5) and had written the former letter in order to help perfect that which was lacking in their faith (I Thess. 3:10). Now, a very short time later, he is able to give thanks for the fact that their faith had grown to a degree beyond his hopes. The verb *groweth exceedingly* is a very strong compound found only here in the New Testament and indicates organic growth as of a healthy plant. Faith always grows as one comes to know more about the One in whom his faith has been placed, and certainly one comes to know the Lord better in times of difficulties. This accounts in part at least for the growth of the Thessalonians' faith. It also grows as one sees the Lord working through him, and this too was true in their case, for theirs was a working faith (1 Thess. 1:3). Persecution helps faith to grow, and a growing faith is a bulwark in times of persecution.

Second, Paul gives thanks for their love (v. 3b). This, too, was an answer to his prayer (I Thess. 3:12). Love is that which seeks the will of God in the one loved, and this the Thessalonians did to all the group. The verb *abound* has a different connotation from the verb *groweth exceedingly* in the first part of the verse. It means "to overspread" as a fire or a flood covers everything in its path. Thus genuine Christian love shed abroad in our hearts by the Holy Spirit (Rom. 5:5) in obedience to the Lord's new commandment (John 13:34) will embrace every other member of the Christian group, not picking and choosing or refusing this or that person. In this instance it overflowed all, even the disorderly idlers. So it should do today in all of our churches.

Because of a growing faith and an expansive love not only were the Thessalonians' hearts kept right in the midst of persecution, but also as a consequence ("so that," v. 4), he was able to boast in all the churches of their constancy under trial. The verb *glory* means "boast" and is an emphatic compound indicating that although it was not Paul's custom to do this, the case of the Thessalonians was so outstanding that even the founder of the church was compelled to sing its praises. It is of their patience and faith that he boasts. Patience means endurance under trial, and faith in this instance probably does not mean faithfulness (as is usually taken to be the meaning of *pistis,* faith, in Gal. 5:22) but faith as in the immediate context. "Tribulations" is a broader word than "persecutions" and includes *any* trouble which a Christian might have. "Persecution" is generally limited to the attacks made on a believer because of his Christian stand. Both tribulations and persecutions continued to be the lot of the Thessalonians, for they were still enduring them when Paul wrote (the verb *endure* is in the present continuous tense).

B. In Persecution Have Your Head Right
1:5-10

Even though the heart is guarded from defection by a growing faith and an abounding love, the head may question the why of having to endure trials. Paul had apparently had a report that some of the believers were beginning to wonder if their difficulties did not deny rather than affirm the righteousness of God. This question he deals with in verses 5 through 10.

Difficulty in understanding the meaning of verse 5 is encountered only if the verse is made to refer to tribulations and persecutions as if they alone were a manifest token of the righteous judgment of God. However, the meaning of the verse is clear if the manifest token of the righteous judgment of God is the endurance and faith of the Thessalonians in the midst of persecutions. Not suffering itself but the attitude of faith and constancy in suffering is the proof cited. In other words, since steadfastness could only be the working of God within the believer (and sometimes it is only in the times of trial that such working of God can be irrefutably demonstrated), this proves that He has in view declaring the believer's worth to be a partaker of the kingdom. The verb *count worthy, kataxioō,* means "to declare or count worthy," not "make worthy" (like *dikaioō,* justify or declare righteous). Thus the Thessalonians are urged to view their endurance as a proof of God's working in them and a guarantee that He will keep His promises concerning their future place in the kingdom.

From this specific deduction Paul moves to certain general statements concerning the judgment of God. Verse 6 states the unassailable fact that God will bring judgment on the wicked and particularly those who were persecuting the Thessalonians. It is an illustration of the principle that whatever a man sows he will reap, for God will pay back with tribulation those who bring tribulation on His people. Verse 7 exhorts the believers to relax in

the knowledge that Christ's coming will be relief
from and righting of every wrong. The verb *rest*
(v. 7) means "relief from tension" or "slackening
of pressure" as one would take down a taut bow
string (cf. Acts 24:23; II Cor. 2:13; 7:5; 8:13 for
the only other uses in the New Testament). Paul
is not saying that the Christian will be free from
trouble until Christ comes, but he does assert that
there can be rest in the midst of trial. And Paul
includes himself in those who are being persecuted
and who enjoy this rest ("with us").

The coming of Christ will bring with it two
things about which these believers needed instruction so that they would be garrisoned in persecution (7b-10). The first is retribution (7b-9). This
happens not only *at* the time of His coming but it
is included *in* it ("when . . ." is literally "in
the revelation . . ." v. 7b). Christ's appearing in
these verses is with great power. He comes from
heaven, accompanied by angels of His power (it
is possible to translate as in the King James Version "mighty angels," but it is better to understand
the genitive in the regular way, "angels of His
power"), and in flaming fire. The latter phrase
continues to describe Christ's person and not His
work. In other words, the flaming fire is the robe
of the Lord in which He appears at His coming.
It is an awesome description of His appearing at

His second coming after the tribulation (cf. Matt. 24:29-31). Vengeance on those who have not obeyed the gospel by receiving the Saviour is meted out at this coming, and it is in the form of everlasting destruction from the presence of the Lord (v. 9). "Shall be punished" means literally "shall pay the penalty," the word *penalty* being from the same root as the word *righteous*. Thus the punishment is not vindictive but deserved. The phrase *everlasting destruction* occurs only here in the New Testament and is everything opposite from eternal life. It is not annihilation but separation from the presence of God and the manifestation of His power. Throughout these verses the power of God is pointedly emphasized to remind the Thessalonians that even though their present adversaries seem powerful there is One who is mightier than all, who will mete out punishment on their tormentors when He appears in great power and glory.

But the second coming of Christ will also be a time of glorification of Christ as well as a time of retribution. Two very amazing statements are contained in verse 10. First, when He comes He will be glorified *in* (not *by*) His saints (the preposition *in* is prefixed to the verb *to be glorified* as well as standing alone after the verb). In other words, Paul is making the astounding claim that the glory

of the Lord will be mirrored in believers (cf.
John 17:1; Eph. 2:7). Only the grace of God can
lift a sinner to the place where He becomes the
means of reflecting the glory of God. Second, Christ
at His coming will be admired or breath-takingly
wondered at in those who believe. Again, Christians are stated to be the ones who bring admiration
to the Lord on the part of those who witness His
return. The spectators of His coming will marvel
greatly at the Lord because they will then see fully
displayed His grace in the completely changed
lives of His people. The world today should see
the same thing to some measure at least in the
lives of Christians as they reflect the grace and
glory of Christ. The parenthesis in verse 10 is
somewhat difficult to interpret, but Paul seems to
be saying that Christ will be admired in all that
believe (and in the Thessalonians too, because his
testimony was believed by them). The general
statement *all that believe* is specifically applied to
the readers in the parenthetical phrase. The
knowledge of that which Christ shall do at His
coming, then, will keep the thoughts of the head
right and bring relaxation in the midst of the trials
of this life.

C. IN PERSECUTION HAVE YOUR HAND RIGHT,
1:11-12

If one's heart is right so that there is spiritual

growth, and if one's head is filled with correct
doctrine, then the hand will be put to proper
tasks, and it is this last thing for which Paul prays
in these closing two verses of the chapter. The
prayer is addressed to God, and its aim is that He
may be able to count or declare the Thessalonians
worthy (cf. on v. 5) of their high calling as Christians. This will be done only if in turn the believers
fulfill all the good pleasure (or good resolve) of
goodness. Notice that the word *his* before *goodness*
is in italics and therefore is not a part of the
original text. Thus the reference is not to the
goodness of God but to the goodness of the Thessalonians, and the clause may be translated, "and
fulfill all the good resolve of doing good." The
fulfilling of the prayer depends on the believers'
having good resolve to do good in this world in
spite of persecution. It is the principle of returning
good for evil. Walking worthy, then, involves
resolving to do good. Coupled with this is "the
work of faith with power." As in I Thessalonians
1:3 faith is not viewed here as merely a passive
thing but as an active use of the power of God in
fruitful service. Thus Paul is praying that even
in the midst of persecution the believers may be
aggressive in performing good works and showing
by their fruits that they serve the living and true
God.

The result of such a life is that the name of
Christ will be glorified (v. 12). The name, of
course, stands for the whole person, so that to
glorify the name of the Lord is to show the world
what the person of the Lord is like. The phrase
and ye in Him emphasizes that close union which
all believers have in Christ, and it is interesting to
note that the doctrine of being in Christ is found
in this early Epistle of Paul's. The Lord first revealed it in John 14:20 (cf. John 15:4-8; 17:1, 10,
21-26). As in the previous verse all of this is
ascribed to the grace of God. It is not within the
power of man to glorify God by his good works;
yet in His grace He condescends to use and em-
power man so that he may perform good works
and glorify his Heavenly Father. This is what
Paul prays God will do through these believers so
that they may walk worthy of their calling particularly in times of trial.

II

CORRECTION CONCERNING
PROPHECY
2:1-17

PAUL DID NOT HESITATE to teach prophecy to
young converts, for I and II Thessalonians are
clear proof of this. Even during his short stay in
Thessalonica he had taught them many of the
details of things to come (II Thess. 2:5), and both
Epistles are filled with allusions to these matters.
However, some had not fully comprehended all
that Paul taught. The fact that some believers had
died without entering the millennial kingdom
became a problem, and Paul deals with this in
I Thessalonians 4:13-18. In the following paragraph (5:1-11) he discusses the Day of the Lord,
which from the Old Testament (to which he refers his readers) includes both the judgment of
the tribulation and the blessing of the millennium.
But it was not the blessed aspect of the Day of the

Lord which confused the believers; rather it was
the judgments at the beginning of that Day about
which they were not clear. In I Thessalonians
5:1-11 Paul tries to make it clear that Christians,
not being appointed to wrath, will escape those
judgments because they will be raptured before the
tribulation begins. Nevertheless, some of the
Thessalonian believers thought that the Day of
the Lord had already come and that they were
living in it because of the persecutions and trials
through which they were passing. It is to this
point, the *coming* of the Day of the Lord, that
Paul speaks in the section before us. He assures
these believers that the Day had not yet come and
would not come until certain other things occur.
Beyond any question believers would not be
subject to the judgments of that Day (for the
meaning of the Day of the Lord see the discussion
at I Thess. 5:1).

A. RELATION OF THE DAY OF THE LORD TO
THE PRESENT, 2:1-2

1. *The Trouble,* 2:1

The subject is set forth in the very first verse —
"the coming of our Lord Jesus Christ and our
gathering together unto Him." This is not an
adjuration, as the King James Version would
imply by translating *huper* "by." *Huper,* the word
translated "by," combines the idea of "concerning"

or "respecting" with "on behalf of." Thus Paul's beseeching is in the interests of the truth of the coming of the Lord and our gathering together unto Him.

The word for "coming," *parousia*, means "presence" and was used by Paul in I Thessalonians 2:19 and 4:15 of the time when the church would be taken to be with Christ before the tribulation begins. Sometimes the word is used of the return of Christ to the earth after the tribulation, but that it does not refer to that latter event here seems clear by the addition of the phrase *and our gathering together unto Him.* "Gathering together" elsewhere in the New Testament is used only in Hebrews 10:25 of the congregating of believers. In this passage it refers to the great congregating of living and sleeping believers in the air to meet their Lord and be with Him forever (1 Thess. 4:13-18). Thus the subject of the passage is clearly stated; it concerns the coming of Christ and in particular that aspect of it which involves our gathering together to meet Him.

2. *The Talk, 2:2*

Word had circulated through the church that the Day of the Lord had already begun, and that meant that the judgments of the beginning of that Day were being experienced by the Thessalonians in the persecutions which they were then enduring.

These false reports had caused a shaking of mind (the meaning of the word *shake* pictures a restless tossing as of a ship, and the aorist tense indicates sudden shock) and continual troubling (the present tense suggests a continuing state of agitation resulting from that sudden shock). The rumors which caused this disturbance had come in three ways. Some were saying that Paul had had a supernatural revelation that the Day of the Lord had already begun. This is the meaning of "by Spirit." (The phrase *as from us* is to be connected with "Spirit," "word," and "letter.") Others either misrepresented or invented a report that Paul had been discoursing on the subject and was proclaiming that the Day of the Lord was here. This is the meaning of "by word." Still others had evidently forged a letter as from Paul, in which it was declared that the Day of the Lord was present. This is probably the meaning of "by letter." Some, however, make this a reference to a misinterpretation of I Thessalonians, but in the light of what is written in II Thessalonians 3:17 it seems more likely that a spurious letter had been circulated.

3. *The Truth,* 2:2b

The truth which Paul affirms emphatically is that the Day of the Lord is not yet present. The King James Version translation, "Day of Christ," is incorrect for it should read "Day of the Lord."

The verb *enestēken* is used elsewhere in the New Testament to mean clearly "to be present" in contrast to something future (Rom. 8:38; I Cor. 3:22). In other words, some were erroneously teaching that some of the events of the many-sided Day of the Lord already had begun to take place. This Paul emphatically denies.

B. RELATION OF THE DAY OF THE LORD TO THE APOSTASY, 2:3a

In order to prove his assertion that the Day of the Lord had not yet begun, Paul first cites the fact that the apostasy which must precede it had not yet appeared. The definite article stands before the word *apostasy*; therefore, Paul is not talking about just any departure from the faith but about a special and well-known one. It is *the* apostasy which will come before the Day of the Lord. *Apostasia*, translated apostasy, does not mean merely disbelieving but rather an aggressive and positive revolt (Acts 21:21; Heb. 3:12). Paul himself later wrote in detail concerning the details of this great departure from the faith in I Timothy 4:1-3 and II Timothy 3:1-5; 4:3-4. In these passages he says that this defection would occur in the last days. It is as though the infidelity of those who profess to be religious will prepare the way and perhaps even furnish the occasion for the final display of revolting against God in the person of the Man of Sin. But the Day of the Lord will not be present until this great apostasy sweeps the earth.[2]

C. RELATION OF THE DAY OF THE LORD TO THE MAN OF SIN, 2:3b-5, 8-10

1. *His Revelation, 2:3b*

Neither will the Day of the Lord begin until the Man of Sin is revealed. This is the event which will begin that awful day of judgment. It is not his existence which is significant; it is his being revealed for what he is, that is, the Man of Sin, which is the signal for the commencement of the events of that Day. Undoubtedly he will have been alive for many years before the Day begins, for he will have grown to manhood before instituting his terrible deeds against God and mankind. But he will be revealed at least to discerning people when he makes a covenant with many of the Jewish people (Dan. 9:27), and this will signal the start of the tribulation period. In this verse he is designated in two ways: the "Man of Sin," which reveals his essential character as unalterably opposed to God; and the "son of perdition," which assures his doom to destruction as Judas, the other son of perdition, experienced (John 17:12; Acts 1:25).

[2]Recently some have interpreted *apostasia* as the departure from the earth, or the rapture of the church. Arguments in support of this can be found in E. Schuyler English, *Re-Thinking the Rapture* (Traveler's Rest, South Carolina: Southern Bible Book House, 1954), pp. 67-71.

Elsewhere in the Bible this same personage is revealed as the "little horn" of Daniel 7:8, the "prince that shall come" of Daniel 9:26, the "willful king" of Daniel 11:36, the "Antichrist who shall come" of I John 2:18, and the "beast out of the sea" of Revelation 13:1-10. While we are warned that there will appear from time to time evil men in the world — and so evil that they may be called antichrists (I John 2:18) — this person is the personification of evil and the culmination of all that is opposed to God.

2. *His Religion*, 2:4-5

In the tribulation days man will not be without religion, for the Man of Sin will furnish his own brand to the world and require people to accept it on penalty of death. He is the one who opposes God (note the link with Satan in I Tim. 5:14 where the same participle is used but translated there "adversary"). He also will exalt himself above God or anything that is called God. The connotation is very broad and is further extended in the phrase *or that is worshiped*. In other words, the Man of Sin will endeavor to take the first place over the true God, any and all false gods, and anything else that man worships. Furthermore, his religious system will be connected with the temple so that he will himself sit in the temple demanding to be worshiped. This is the abomination of deso-

lation spoken of by Daniel (9:27) and attested to
by our Lord (Matt. 24:15) which will stand in
the holy place requiring the worship of men.

All of this Paul had taught the Thessalonians
when he was in their midst. The verb *told* in
verse 5 is in the imperfect tense, which indicates
that he repeatedly told them of these matters
relative to the second coming. This ought to be
an encouragement to any who might feel timid
about teaching prophecy to new converts.

3. *His Power,* 2:9-10

In verses 9 and 10 there are a number of very
descriptive words which vividly portray the power
of the Antichrist. In general, his power and activity
may be described as a counterfeiting. He too will
have a *parousia,* coming, as will the Lord (v. 9).
He also will be empowered (analagous to the
Lord's being filled with the Spirit during His
earthly ministry) — except that the Man of Sin's
power will come from Satan (cf. Rev. 13:4). He
will perform counterfeit miracles. They will be
"in power" (cf. Luke 4:36); they will have meaning, for they are called signs (cf. John 2:11); and
they will have the effect on people of being
"wonders of lying" (cf. John 4:48; Acts 2:22), i.e.,
things which cannot be explained. These will promote deceit (this is the word which is translated
"deceivableness" in v. 10) which originates from

the unrighteousness of the Man of Sin and his program. All of this will be perpetrated on those who are perishing, simply because they would not receive the truth and be saved. How widespread and how mighty will be this evil man's power to counterfeit the truth that is in Christ and His gospel.

4. *His Punishment, 2:8*

Underlying this entire section which so vividly describes the power of the Man of Sin is the firm note of the sovereign and almighty power of God. This is clearly seen in verse 8, where Paul describes the destruction of the Man of Sin. The place of his doom has already been mentioned as perdition (v. 3). Here the means of bringing it to pass is described as by "the spirit [or breath] of His mouth." This expression occurs only here in the New Testament and indicates a "sweeping away like a hurricane, or killing like the blast from a furnace" (Plummer, *A Commentary on St. Paul's Second Epistle to the Thessalonians,* p. 64). Parallel to this idea is the expression in the last part of the verse *the brightness of His coming.* The very appearance of the Lord will effect the destruction. In reality, however, the "destroying" of the Man of Sin is not annihilation. It is a putting out of business, for the verb translated "destroy" actually means "to make idle" or "render inoperative" (cf.

Rom. 6:6). The Man of Sin will be destroyed in this sense by being cast alive into the lake of fire (Rev. 19:20), and he will remain alive in that place for all eternity (cf. Rev. 20:10). This is his certain punishment, and it is as sure as the power of God.

D. RELATION OF THE DAY OF THE LORD TO THE RESTRAINER, 2:6-7

Verse 8 begins with a word that indicates sequence of events — *tote,* then. It stands in sharp contrast to "now" in verse 6 and "already" and "now" in verse 7. When the restrainer is taken out of the way *then* the Man of Sin will be revealed. We have already been told that the Day of the Lord cannot begin until the Man of Sin is revealed, and since the Man of Sin cannot be revealed until the restrainer is removed, it follows that the Day of the Lord cannot begin either until the restrainer is removed. Paul distinguishes this order of events very clearly.

Not only is the order of events apparent, but so also is the work of the restrainer. It is described by the word *withhold.* This word can mean "hold fast" (as in I Thess. 5:21) or "hold back" (as here and Rom. 1:18). The restrainer holds back the full manifestation of evil in the person of the Man of Sin, and that is why the Man of Sin cannot be revealed until the restrainer be removed. That evil is already at work is affirmed in verse 7, but its full revelation awaits the appearance of the Man of Sin.

The thing that is debated in these verses is the identification of the restrainer. In verse 6 "what withholdeth" is a neuter participle with the neuter article. In verse 7 "he who withholds" is a masculine participle with the masculine article. Furthermore, Paul says that the Thessalonians were acquainted with what it is that restrains (v. 6). Finally, there is one other fact so often overlooked; namely, the restrainer must be more powerful than Satan who empowers the Man of Sin in order to hold back this evil one. Thus the facts in the text tell us that the restrainer is a principle and a person, that the identification was well known to the readers, and that the power of the restrainer must be greater than Satan's. Most commentators identify the restrainer with the Roman Empire of Paul's day, which held back evil by its advanced system of laws, many of which are still basic to legal systems in our day (cf. Findlay, pp. 177-179). It is admitted, however, by those who hold this view that the restrainer is not merely the Roman Empire but government in general, since it is only too apparent that the Man of Sin did not make his appearance at the end of the Roman Empire (cf. Morris, pp. 129-130). Support for this view is cited from Paul's own statement that governments are ordained of God for the purpose of restraining evil (Rom. 13:1-7). However, it must be recognized that governments do not always fulfill their ordained purpose, and furthermore no government is stronger in power than Satan himself. It should also be remembered that the tribulation period during which the Man of Sin holds sway is a time of super-government.

Other suggestions for the identity of the restrainer include Satan (but verse 7 precludes this interpretation), some powerful angel (but Jude 9, which shows the impotence of the archangel in the face of Satanic opposition, argues against this), or no positive identification at all. It is sometimes asserted that Paul himself was unsure (but how did the Thessalonians know if Paul did not teach them, vv. 5-6?), or more often that even though Paul and his readers knew, we who read this letter today cannot know.

Ultimately a decision as to the identity of the restrainer will be made on the basis of answering the question, Who is powerful enough to hold back Satan? The obvious and only answer to that question is God. Therefore, the restrainer must be God Himself. In this view the neuter in verse 6 would remind us of the power of God in general, and the masculine in verse 7 would point to the

person of God. Most premillennialists further
identify the restrainer as the third person of the
Godhead, the Holy Spirit (cf. Walvoord, *The
Rapture Question,* pp. 86-87). In this regard it
may be suggested that the use of the neuter in
verse 6 is to be accounted for by the fact that the
Greek word for *Spirit* is itself neuter.The masculine in verse 7 is explained as indicative of the
truth that the Spirit is a person who should be
referred to in the masculine gender (as is done in
John 15:26; 16:13-14; Eph. 1:13-14). The fact that
one of the first specific indications of the work of
the Holy Spirit is that of restraining (Gen. 6:3)
adds support to this interpretation.

It is extremely difficult to see how the restrainer
can be anyone other than God Himself. Undoubtedly God uses good government, elect angels, and
other means to restrain evil, but the ultimate
power behind such forceful restraint must be the
power of God and the person of God. This much
appears to be beyond question. Whether Paul is
specifically referring to the Holy Spirit in this
passage (though it is recognized that restraining is
elsewhere said to be His work) may be debatable.
However, it should be clearly recognized that
whether or not this further identification of the
restrainer as the Spirit is made does not affect the

argument for a pretribulation rapture of the church.

That pretribulation argument is simply this. The restrainer is God, and the instrument of restraint is the God-indwelt church (cf. Eph. 4:6 for God indwelling; Gal. 2:20 for Christ indwelling; I Cor. 6:19 for the Spirit indwelling). It should be remembered that Christ said of the divinely indwelt and empowered church that "the gates of hell shall not prevail against it" (Matt. 16:18), so we can say that this indwelt, empowered church is an adequate restraining instrument against the forces of darkness. The church will not go through any of the tribulation because the restrainer will be removed before the Man of Sin is revealed, which revelation (with the signing of the covenant with the Jews, Dan. 9:27) begins the tribulation period. Since the restrainer is ultimately God, and since God indwells all Christians, either He must be withdrawn from the hearts of believers while they are left on earth to go through the tribulation, or else when He is withdrawn all believers are taken with Him. Since it is impossible for a believer to be "disindwelt" the only alternative is that believers too will be taken out of the way before the appearance of the Man of Sin, which signals the start of the tribulation.

Against this interpretation it is usually argued

that "it is difficult to see in what sense either [the Father or the Spirit] could *be taken out of the way* (verse 7)" (Morris, p. 130). The answer to this lies in the difference of meaning between *residence* and *presence.* Every person of the Godhead has been, is, and always will be present in the world simply because God is omnipresent. But the persons of the Godhead and particularly the Holy Spirit have not always been resident within the hearts of God's people either permanently or universally (see John 14:17, where the preposition *with* describes the relationship of the Holy Spirit in the Old Testament, while the preposition *in* describes it in the New Testament). Today God has bound Himself to be resident within the hearts of all of His people and always (cf. Rom. 8:9; I Cor. 6:19). Thus, to say that the restrainer is removed is not to say that the presence of God is taken away from the earth, nor is it to imply that God (or specifically the Holy Spirit) will cease to work in the world in any way including the work of regeneration. Many will be saved in the tribulation period (cf. Rev. 7:14), and God will be the One who accomplishes that work just as He did in Old Testament times. God's universal and permanent residence in His people is a distinctive relationship in this day of grace, and certainly the removal of His residence (including those believers in whom He resides) does not mean the withdrawal of His presence or the cessation of His activity. No other interpretation does full justice to all the facts and implications of this passage.

E. RELATION OF THE DAY OF THE LORD TO UNBELIEVERS, 2:10-12

In the middle of verse 10 the spotlight is put on those who follow the Man of Sin and believe his lie. Because they receive not the truth, they perish (the participle is in the present tense, indicating that they are already perishing even though they are yet alive). Verses 11 and 12 set forth the consequence of this unbelief, the opening phrase *and for this cause* pointing back to verse 10. It is that God sends strong delusion. The two words translated "strong delusion" mean literally "a powerful working of error," and the sending of it is attributed to God. It might seem that this sending of delusion ought to be the work of Satan, but it is the sovereign God who inflicts it on man because he did not receive the truth when he had the chance. The purpose of the delusion is that men may believe "the" (not "a," because the definite article is in the original text) lie of Satan as proclaimed by the Man of Sin. All men are believers in something, and in these future days they will either believe the truth of God or believe the lie of Satan. A second purpose of God's

sending the strong delusion is stated in verse 12 —
that all such unbelievers may be condemned. The
justification for their judgment is simply that they
believed not the truth and rejoiced in iniquity. It
is a picture of lowest degradation and complete
opposition to God and His truth. The Man of Sin
may have widespread success for a time, but it is
God who will ultimately triumph over all evil.

F. RELATION OF THE DAY OF THE LORD
TO THE BELIEVER, 2:13-17

In this last paragraph of the chapter, Paul turns
from the awful contemplation of Antichrist and
the doom of his followers to the bright prospect
that belongs to the Thessalonians and all believers
everywhere. Again as in 1:3 his thoughts are cast
in the form of a thanksgiving made necessary because of what God had done in their hearts.

1. *The Believer's Position,* 2:13-14

Two things are said about a believer's position
which are the basis for his prospect. He has been
chosen (v. 13) and called (v. 14). The word
which Paul uses to describe the choosing is an
unusual one and is used nowhere else in the New
Testament of divine election (though it is used
otherwise in Phil. 1:22 and Heb. 11:25). In the
Greek Old Testament it is used in relation to
God's choosing Israel (Deut. 26:18). The time
when this choosing was done is said to be the

"beginning." Some understand this to mean the beginning of the preaching mission in Thessalonica, but it is better to see "from the beginning" as a reference to the beginning of all things; i.e., from before the world began. This is an idea which is regularly found in Paul's writings (I Cor. 2:7; Eph. 1:4). God had the choice of His people in mind in eternity past. The end purpose of the choosing was salvation, and this was accomplished "through sanctification of the Spirit and belief of the truth." In this phrase the divine and human responsibilities in salvation are seen together. On God's part, being saved involves the work of the Holy Spirit in sanctifying or setting apart the believer. This is a reference to that sanctification of position which every Christian has the moment he believes (I Cor. 6:11, ASV) The human responsibility is to believe the truth, and the two aspects are linked inseparably, as shown by the single occurrence of the preposition *in*.

While the choosing of verse 13 is in eternity, the calling of verse 14 is related to time. It was accomplished through the preaching of the gospel and involves the obtaining of glory in a future day (cf. 1:10). There is a great deal of deep theology bound up in the simple statements of these two verses, and like all theology it had its practical use — in this case encouraging the Thessalonians in their difficulties and trials.

2. *The Believer's Practice,* 2:15-17

Therefore — since believers were included in the pre-temporal purpose of God and are guaranteed ultimately the glory of God, and since believers cannot be overcome by Satan or his Man of Sin — therefore, stand fast in the midst of opposition from the enemies of Christ and in the face of uncertainty of the time of the return of Christ. Furthermore, believers are exhorted to hold fast the traditions of Christ. The word *traditions* does not mean things which men have made up but merely something which has been passed on from one to another and which was received in the first place from God Himself. "The prominent idea of *paradosis* [tradition] then in the New Testament is that of an authority external to the teacher himself" (Lightfoot, *Notes on Epistles of St. Paul,* p. 121). These teachings from God were handed on by word and by letter (I Cor. 11:2; II Thess. 3:6; cf. Rom. 6:17; I Cor. 15:3; II Tim. 1:13), and whether by letter or word they were authoritative.

The section closes with prayer for strength to stand fast and hold fast the traditions. It invokes the help of Christ and the Father who loved us (as exhibited at Calvary) and who has given everlasting consolation (which word includes the idea of strength) and good hope based on the grace of God. The help comes in the form of comfort and establishing (v. 17). Here too the word *comfort* has the idea of strength. Strength and stability in every good word and work is that which is requested. "It is the rousing and cheering of the whole inner man which the Apostles pray for, — that the Thessalonians may be animated to brave endurance and vigorous activity" (Findlay, p. 194).

Summing up the thrust of this chapter, it is simply this: Do not be disturbed for the Day of the Lord has not yet come. When it does come it will be a terrible time of revealing the power of Satan through his Man of Sin. But you believers will not experience these awful things, for your prospect is glory, not wrath. In the meantime, however, maintain a strong and stable Christian testimony in every word and work.

III

CORRECTION CONCERNING
PRACTICE
3:1-15

MOST OF PAUL'S EPISTLES can be divided into two main sections, doctrinal and practical. This one is no exception, and the first word of chapter 3 indicates that the principal doctrinal argument is closed and that whatever follows, however weighty and important, is nonetheless incidental to the main argument. "Finally" signals the beginning of the end (as I Thess. 4:1).

The chapter opens with a request for prayer (vv. 1-2), a word of encouragement concerning the faithfulness of God (vv. 3-4), and a short prayer (v. 5). The request for prayer is in the present tense in verse 1 and evidently means that Paul had heard that the Thessalonians were praying for him, and he asks them to keep on doing it. His request is twofold. First, he asks them to keep on

119

praying that the gospel may have a rapid and triumphant course. "Have free course" translates
the single word *run*. Both "run" and "be glorified"
are in the present tense, signifying that the request
is for a continuously swift advance and success of
the word of the Lord. The second petition is for
deliverance (v. 2). That Paul had in mind a specific
situation in which he needed deliverance and not
merely a general deliverance from all enemies of
the gospel is indicated by two things. The verb
delivered is in the aorist tense, which points to
a particular deliverance, and the definite article
occurs before "unreasonable and wicked men." In
other words, Paul is asking for deliverance from
the particular enemies who were giving him
trouble at that time. The reference must be to
the Jews who were giving him trouble at that
time, — to the Jews who opposed the apostle's
ministry in Corinth (Acts 18:1-18). The last phrase
in the verse, "for all men have not faith," reminds
his readers that opposition is to be expected simply
because not all are believers.

Verses 3 and 4 give a word of encouragement
concerning the faithfulness of Christ in contrast to
the lack of faith in those referred to in verse 2. Not
all have faith, but faithful is the Lord "who will
establish you." We might have expected Paul to
say "establish us" but his first concern is always for ·

his converts. He also assures them that God's faithfulness will keep them from "evil." The form of the word *evil* can be either masculine (the evil one, Satan) or neuter (evil things). Probably we are to understand it as a reference to Satan here in light of Paul's previous concern as expressed in I Thessalonians 3:5. His confidence in the faithfulness of God also extends to their keeping his commandments, both those which he had given them and those which he was about to give them in verses 6 through 15. It is a tactful way to introduce what follows.

This expression of confidence in God leads Paul to breathe a short prayer which concludes these introductory verses to the chapter. It is one of those very few prayers in the New Testament addressed to the Lord Jesus (cf. Acts 7:60), and it concerns two things about the inner lives of the Thessalonian believers. First, Paul prays that their hearts may be directed into the love of God. If the genitive "of God" is subjective it means our love for God, and if it is objective it means His love for us. Possibly here both ideas are included (Lightfoot, pp. 127-128); thus Paul prays that the believers may realize fully what God's love for them means and in return love Him more. Second, Paul prays that their hearts may be directed into the steadfastness (not patient waiting, but endurance

as in I Thess. 1:3) of Christ. In other words, he is
asking that they might reproduce the endurance
in the face of trials which Christ exhibited in His
own life on earth.

A.   THE DISORDERLY ONES,
3:6-13

Next to the section concerning the Day of the
Lord in chapter 2 this is the longest in the Epistle.
It shows how aggravated the problem of laziness
had become since the writing of I Thessalonians
(cf. 4:11-12; 5:14). Doctrinal misconception always
results in practical misconduct. Misunderstanding
the truths involved in Christ's second coming had
led some to expect that they would not have to
work any more until the Lord came. Paul's admonitions in the first letter had not nipped the
problem in the bud; thus this lengthy and extremely authoritative section.

1.   *The Penalty for the Disorderly, 3:6*

The erring brethren are designated as those who
walk disorderly. This is a military term and means
"those out of rank." Concerning such Paul gives
command "in the name of our Lord Jesus Christ."
This expression is as authoritative as Paul can
make it, and yet at the same time Paul recognizes
the disorderly person as a "brother." The command
is to withdraw from the brother who is out of
rank. The word *withdraw* is used elsewhere in the

New Testament in II Corinthians 8:20 only, but it pictures the furling of sails or the gathering together of a robe as a sign of disgust. It is not a withdrawal with an air of superiority, but it is an aloofness which signifies no condoning of the deeds of the disorderly.

2. *The Pattern for the Disorderly, 3:7-9*

The disorderliness in these verses is not general and unspecific but refers particularly to the failure to earn one's living. Paul reminds his readers again (cf. I Thess. 1:6; 2:3) of his own example in this regard and exhorts them to follow (literally, "imitate") him. Indeed it is more than an exhortation that is stated in verse 7 — it is an obligation that is imposed. Paul's example is of hard work (v. 8) which included night work in order that he would not have to be dependent on anyone else for his support. It is also an example of humble willingness (v. 9), for he reminds them that although he had the right to receive financial support from them, he waived that right in order to set a good example for them.

3. *The Precept for the Disorderly, 3:10*

The clear-cut rule which Paul laid down when he was with them was this: "If any will not work, let him not eat." This may have been a common saying of the day which Paul simply took over and gave spiritual sanction to.

4. *The Pursuits for the Disorderly,* 3:11-13

Particular cases had evidently been reported to Paul and he now mentions them, though anonymously, in these verses. These people were pursuing the wrong occupation. They were busybodies instead of being busy. There is a neat play on the Greek words in verse 11 since the word *busybody* is built on the root of the word *work*. The adjectival form for "busybody" is found in I Timothy 5:13. Probably these brethren were busily trying to convert others to the idea that they too should quit working in view of the nearness of the Lord's return. Instead they should have been working so that they could support themselves (v. 12). This should be accompanied with an inner quietness replacing the state of agitation they were in over the second coming. Finally, to all Paul says "be not weary in well doing" (v. 13). "Be not weary" means "do not lose heart" (cf. Luke 18:1; II Cor. 4:1, 16; Gal 6:9 for the only other occurrences), and "well-doing" means doing the noble thing. However long the Lord may delay His coming, and whatever disorderliness others may engage in, we should constantly conduct ourselves according to the highest standards and do it without flagging.

B. THE DISOBEDIENT ONES, 3:14-15

Paul, remembering how his former admonition

had been neglected, now directs the church as to what to do in case the more obstinate offenders disregarded his present commands. His advice is threefold. First, the disobedient one is to be noted (v. 14). The verb *note* has the connotation of marking something well or branding. In other words, the church is to mark off with disapproval any one who does not obey what Paul wrote in this letter. Though the command to brand such a one is clear, the means of doing it is not stated. Perhaps it involved some sort of congregational censure.

Second, the believers were to "have no company" with one who disobeyed these commands (v. 14). This verb literally means "don't mix yourselves up with him." It prohibits familiar fellowship in order that, being cut off from the company of fellow-believers, the disobedient one may be ashamed. The object of this isolation of the erring brother is remedial, not vindictive.

Third, the sinning brother is to be admonished. The verb means "to put in mind of the truth." The purpose of this treatment of the disobedient one is to restore him to fellowship, and that is why Paul insists that the church remember that the person they are dealing with is a brother in the Lord. Perhaps he feared that some would be over-zealous to take too drastic action, and, of course, it goes without saying that when the offender confesses his wrong he is to be forgiven and restored.

The Epistle concludes with a prayer (v. 16), a salutation (v. 17), and a benediction (v. 18). The prayer is for tranquility of heart, and it had evidently come to Paul's mind because of the things he had just been discussing. It is only the Lord of peace who can give peace in the midst of trials and restlessness concerning the second coming. This peace for which Paul prays is one which will remain continually ("always"), which will not vary in spite of altering circumstances ("by all means"), and which comes to the heart because of the presence of the Lord with us ("the Lord be with you all").

The salutation of verse 17 is written by Paul's own hand, for as was his custom, he dictated the letter to a secretary who wrote it down. But at the conclusion he himself takes the pen and adds a few words in his own handwriting (cf. Gal. 6:11). This was a sign of genuineness and was particularly needed in this Epistle because of the forged letter which had been circulated in Paul's name (2:2).

The letter concludes with a customary benediction and one that was especially gracious in this instance, for it encompassed all the believers, even the ones whom Paul had rebuked in the Epistle. The great apostle's heart always went out to all his flock.

BIBLIOGRAPHY

Deissmann, Adolf. *New Light on the New Testament.* Edinburgh: T. & T. Clark, 1907.

English, E. Schuyler. *Re-Thinking the Rapture.* Traveler's Rest, South Carolina: Southern Bible Book House, 1954.

Findlay, G. G. *The Epistles of Paul the Apostle to the Thessalonians. (Cambridge Greek Testament)* Cambridge: The University Press, 1911.

Hogg, C. F., and Vine, W. E. *The Epistles of Paul the Apostle to the Thessalonians.* Glasgow: Pickering & Inglis, [n. d.].

Lightfoot, J. B. *Notes on Epistles of St. Paul from unpublished commentaries.* London: Macmillan and Co., 1895.

Milligan, George. *St Paul's Epistles to the Thessalonians.* Grand Rapids, Michigan: Wm. B. Eerdmans Publishing Company, 1952.

Morris, Leon. *The Epistles of Paul to the Thessalonians.* Grand Rapids, Michigan: Wm. B. Eerdmans Publishing Company, 1957.

Plummer, Alfred. *A Commentary on St. Paul's First Epistle to the Thessalonians.* London: Robert Scott, 1918.

————. *A Commentary on St. Paul's Second Epistle to the Thessalonians.*

Ramsay, W. M. *St. Paul the Traveller and the Roman Citizen.* London: Hodder and Stoughton, 1895.

Robinson, J. Armitage. *St. Paul's Epistle to the Ephesians.* London: Macmillan and Co., Limited, 1914.

Salmon, George. *A Historical Introduction to the Study of the Books of the New Testament.* London: John Murray, 1892.

Walvoord, John F. *The Rapture Question.* Findlay, Ohio: Dunham Publishing Company, 1957.